ROBERT BAKER OF PICCADILLY HALL
AND HIS HEIRS

ROBERT BAKER OF PICCADILLY HALL
AND HIS HEIRS

Francis Sheppard

London Topographical Society

Publication no. 127

1982

Dedicated to Martin Holmes Esquire, FSA,
of Appleby in the County of Westmorland
and formerly Assistant Keeper of the London Museum

QUEEN MARY
COLLEGE
LIBRARY

© Francis Sheppard 1982

Publication no. 127 of the
London Topographical Society
3 Meadway Gate, London NW11

PRINTED IN GREAT BRITAIN BY
DAEDALUS PRESS, WISBECH, CAMBRIDGESHIRE

Contents

Illustrations

Preface

In the course of preparing volume XXXI of the *Survey of London*, published in 1963, I had occasion to look into the early history of Piccadilly, and a short account of the matter was included in that volume. But I added that 'elements of uncertainty still remain . . . to challenge future research'.

The present study is the result of subsequent inquiries which I made to satisfy my own curiosity. I should like to thank the following for their generous help; the staffs of the Public Record Office and of the Somerset Record Office; Mr Noel Blakiston, formerly Assistant Keeper at the Public Record Office, whose own curiosity about 'The Origin of Piccadilly' led him, as long ago as 1944, to publish important new evidence on the matter, and who twenty years later gave me invaluable assistance at the Public Record Office; and Mr Martin Holmes, formerly Assistant Keeper at the London Museum, who read my first draft and with his habitual persuasiveness made numerous suggestions. Finally, I am most grateful of all to the members of the Council of the London Topographical Society for undertaking to publish this essay; and in particular to their Honorary Editor, Mrs Ann Saunders, for promoting the project with her unfailing enthusiasm over a number of years.

FRANCIS SHEPPARD

I *Robert Baker the Taylor*

In 1866 several students of etymology rushed into print in support of Archdeacon Bicker-steth's idea that the name Piccadilly was a corruption of 'peaked hill'.[1] Sporadic discussion of the origin of the word had already been going on for over two hundred years. Thomas Blount had started the argument in a dictionary which he published in 1656. By that time the pickadils worn in the time of Elizabeth and James I had gone out of fashion, and so he began with a definition of this obsolete article of dress. A 'Pickadil', wrote Blount, was 'the round hem, or the several divisions set together about the skirt of a Garment; or other thing; also a kinde of stiff collar, made in fashion of a Band'. Then he went on to make two suggestions about the origin of Piccadilly the place-name — 'Hence perhaps that famous Ordinary [i.e., eating-house] near St. James called Pickadilly, took denomination; because it was then the outmost or skirt house of the Suburbs that way. Others say it took name from this, that one Higgins, a Tailor, who built it, got most of his Estate by Pickadilles, which in the last age were much worn in England.'[2]

These suggestions were very near the truth, but Blount had mistaken the name of the tailor who had made his fortune from the sale of pickadils. Almost two centuries elapsed before Peter Cunningham examined the records of the parish of St Martin in the Fields and found that the tailor who built Piccadilly Hall was not 'one Higgins' but one Robert Baker.[3] Blount had now been proved wrong about the identity of the tailor, so everything else that he had said was presumed to be wrong too, and Archdeacon Bickersteth could muse about peaked hills, unchallenged in his Buckinghamshire rectory. Nobody thought of trying to find out more about either Higgins or Robert Baker, and in 1925 C. L. Kingsford even stated that Higgins had proved to be a myth.[4] But in 1944 Mr Noel Blakiston found evidence at the Public Record Office that Higgins, far from being a myth, had been a very lively apothecary living in the Savoy, and that Robert Baker had been his son-in-law.[5] In 1963 a short account of the Bakers of Piccadilly was published in the *Survey of London*, but a great deal of the story still remained undiscovered.[6]

Biographies of obscure people about whom not much is known usually begin with a tedious inquisition into the subjects' ancestry. So the account of Robert Baker begins with the conventional statement that he was born in the county of Somerset in the early years of the reign of Queen Elizabeth, of poor and presumably honest parents.[7] But in Baker's case this was of vital importance, for a century later the fate of his great estate depended solely upon the evidence which his descendants could produce about his

9

place of origin and parentage. They ransacked the parish registers and manorial court rolls for information about his birth, marriage, family and death, and in 1658 and 1663 clever London lawyers went down to Somerset to examine ancient men and women who knew anything about him. They questioned people in London, too, and in the Court of Chancery in Westminster Hall they continued to debate for more than ten years until the matter was decided. By a final decree the Court of Chancery determined Robert Baker's ancestry and hence the identity of his rightful heir; and the Court of Chancery, one might suppose, could hardly have been wrong.

Much of the written evidence which was produced in Chancery still exists. The registers of baptisms, marriages and burials for St Mary Magdalene, Taunton, are still kept in the parish where the contenders for Robert Baker's estate so diligently searched them three hundred years ago. The Somerset Record Office now houses the court rolls of the Manor of Taunton Priory and Canon Street, the registers for St John's, Staplegrove, and much else besides, and at the Public Record Office there are the voluminous archives of the formidable Court of Chancery itself, including the evidence taken in 1658 and 1663. The testimony of the illiterate old men and women who were examined then is almost valueless for the dates of the events they were questioned about – when asked how old they were some of them could only reply 'fowerscore yeares or there-abouts' [8] – but the touchingly inconsequent details and above all the scraps of conversation which they dredged from the depths of the memory of their far-off youth convey far greater conviction than more sophisticated testimony. Their recollections are often the only source for much of Robert Baker's career, but occasionally it has been possible to check the truth of their statements from other records. Gradually the story of the Bakers of Piccadilly emerges – comic, pathetic and confused, but reasonably complete at last.

In 1570 Robert Baker's father, William Baker, a merchant dealing in cloth and corn, was living at Staplegrove in Somerset. Staplegrove is about three-quarters of a mile north-west of Taunton, the outer tentacles of which now extend to within two or three fields of the village. There is a little mediaeval church with a low tower, dominated by a great dark cedar. The churchyard is full of weathered eighteenth-century tombstones, and in one corner is the village school, built over a century ago and still in use. Across the road is a farmstead, and away to the south, beyond the Vale of Taunton, are the Blackdown Hills.

Between 1568 and 1571 William Baker's wife bore him three sons.[9] Shortly afterwards he appears to have removed to a house in Canon Street, Taunton, where, evidently, a fourth son, Robert, was born, perhaps in 1578 or 1579.[10] Robert probably received no schooling, for in 1599 he could not sign his name, and had to inscribe his initials to a deed of surrender. Even this was difficult for him, for the R is written back to front, and it may be that he never learned to write easily.[11]

William Baker died in 1584. He left a good estate, which was later described as 'divers goods, chattels, household stuffe, money and plate' to the value of over £300, as well as his house in Canon Street. His wife was already dead, and there was no one to look after his five surviving children – William, Robert and three daughters – all of them still under age. In accordance with the custom of the Bishop of Winchester's Manor of Taunton, the house in Canon Street passed to his youngest surviving son, Robert, and in his will he distributed his movable property between his eldest son, also William, who was made sole executor, and his three daughters.[12]

William the son was only thirteen years of age, and it was not long before the proverbial wicked uncle, another Robert Baker, who lived in Bridgwater, and three accomplices descended upon the helpless orphans.[13] Before any inventory of the estate could be made they conveyed away ('by night in verie secrett manner') a great part of William Baker senior's goods, including 'divers lynnene, monie, silver spones, bondes, bills and specialties, haye, Stamell Cloath, other Cloath of divers other Cullers, Corne, Malte and other things'. Then they made an inventory of what was left, which they valued at 'verie small Rate', and applied (apparently unsuccessfully) to obtain probate of the will.[14]

After this disaster young William Baker turned to and provided for his brother and sisters, soon setting himself up as a mercer or linen draper in 'a certaine house between the red Lyon and the Beare'. Neither of these inns survive, but the Bear was on the east side of North Street, at or near the site of the British Home Stores. Whether Robert was apprenticed to his brother or was merely his servant is not clear – in practice there was probably little difference. He was brought up with William's own young family (William married in 1591) and travelled to the markets round Taunton to help sell his brother's wares.[8]

It was while he was still living in Taunton that young Robert first began to work as a tailor. He is said to have 'wrought with one Mr. Tankynes, a Taylor in Taunton, as a journeyman', and Tankynes' (or Tompkins') daughter remembered that Robert had been 'a servant unto and wrought with' her father 'for some tyme'. It seems that he never served a full seven-year apprenticeship.[15]

At this point the chronology of events becomes extremely vague, and the only certainty, upon which all the evidence agrees, is that while still a young man Robert left his native county and went to London to work as a tailor. Townsmen of Taunton often went to London to sell woollen stuffs, this commercial connexion being greatly helped by the ease with which holders of copyhold land in the Bishop of Winchester's Manor of Taunton could raise capital on a mortgage. Thus an enterprising tradesman could 'go to London and sell his stuffs, and return down his moneys, and pay but five pounds in the hundred for his moneys, and discharge his lands. This is the cause of the great trade and riches about Taunton-Dean'.[16]

Robert may have been encouraged to go to London by a friend or relative. He probably travelled by waggon, or with a string of packhorses, and the journey of 145 miles must have taken at least a week. He had evidently decided to make use of his experience as a tailor with Mr Tompkins at Taunton, for we are told that 'hee fell to worke upon his said trade of a Taylor as soon as he came to London for himselfe'. Years later an old man named Paul Bettering recalled that Robert had 'wrought as a Journeyman att Mr. Brales ye Taylor . . . upon his first coming to London'. Mr Brales lived at the sign of the Flying Horse in the Strand, and Bettering claimed that he had worked there with Baker and 'other journeymen tailors that were Somersettshire men . . . to clubb with them'.[17]

Later on several people declared that soon after his arrival in London Baker served in the army at Tilbury during the threat of Spanish invasion in 1588. Elizabeth Andrews, whose father had been a business friend of Robert Baker's, said that she had heard that Baker had been 'a souldier att Tilburie Camp'. William Robinson of St Marylebone, yeoman, and his wife Elizabeth were more specific. They declared that Elizabeth's father, William Nicholls or Nicholson, had worked as a tailor with Baker in the Strand, and that they 'were both of them souldiers together att Tilburie Campe, beinge but new married men when they went out with the Earle of Essex thither'.[17]

Baker was certainly not a married man in 1588, and if he was indeed born in 1578 or 1579, as has been suggested earlier, he cannot have seen military service during the Armada crisis. But it is possible that he was not much younger than his elder brother William, who was born at Staplegrove in 1571, and in that case he could have served, for all able-bodied men between the ages of sixteen and sixty were liable for service with the militia; and he could certainly have served, as William and Elizabeth Robinson also affirmed, 'in Cales Vioiage', by which they meant the capture of Cadiz under the Earl of Essex in 1596.[17]

The 1590's are, indeed, the most obscure years in the whole of Robert Baker's career, perhaps because he spent some time abroad. A lawsuit in the Court of Requests shows that in 1595 one Robert Bahere of London, feltmaker, had 'dealings for land, wares and merchandise' with Christopher Robinson, a leatherseller. Bahere, being about to 'travell beyond the seas', had sold 'certeyn howses' to Robinson, who had entreated him to 'travayle to Callis [Calais] in France, theire to receyve certeyne goods' of Robinson's. The upshot of these transactions was a dispute about outstanding debts.[18] Perhaps Robert Bahere and Robert Baker were two different people; Bahere is nevertheless such a very odd name that it might be a copyist's error, and complicated deals in 'land, wares and merchandise' were Robert Baker's particular speciality a few years later. There was certainly a tradition that he had lived abroad, learned his trade in France, and made a great deal of money 'by adventuring as a Merchant beyond the seas'.[19]

In 1599 Robert Baker sold his cottage in Canon Street, Taunton, to John French, from whom, perhaps, French Weir in Taunton takes its name. The deed of surrender was entered on the manorial court rolls, and Baker signed it with his initials – the only surviving example of his hand.[11] Evidently he now had no intention of ever returning to live in Taunton, and needed capital to set up his own home in London, for on 16 November 1600 he married Elizabeth Nightingale at St Martin in the Fields.[20]

After their marriage the Bakers went to live in St Martin's Lane. Elizabeth Andrews, who at that time was a little girl of ten, said in 1658 that she could remember Robert 'ever since shee could well remember any thing', and that he had lived 'within foare dores or thereabouts' of her father's house, also in St Martin's Lane. Baker's bride was described by several witnesses as a flaxwoman. Jane Jeames, who when a girl had been a servant at Robert Baker's house at Piccadilly, said that Mrs Baker had been 'a verie Carefull good woman and wiffe to him'. Care in domestic matters was very important, for Robert was still 'but a poore Countrey Taylor when hee marryed his said first wife ye Flaxwoman . . .'.[17] And nine months after the marriage a son, Robert, was born. He was christened at St Martin in the Fields on 6 August 1601, but only survived a few days and was buried on 13 August. A year later a daughter, Frances, was born, and was christened on 26 August 1602.[21]

Fortune came at last to Robert Baker in the Strand, to which he moved from St Martin's Lane within about three years of his marriage.[22] Here he lived at the sign of the Seven Stars, where in the words of Anne Smith he and his wife 'kept a flax shoppe between ye new Exchange and Yorke House'. Anne Smith's father had lived nearby, 'over against ye Seaven Starrs', and Anne could remember Baker in the Strand since 'shee was a girle or could well Remember any thing'. Her recollection was confirmed by several other neighbours, and by the first appearance of Robert Baker's name as the payer of two shillingsworth of rates in the parish overseers' accounts for 1603-4.[23]

What Elizabeth Andrews later described as Baker's 'poore little shoppe in ye Strand' stood on the river or south side of the street in York Rents, somewhere between Villiers Street and George Court. Here stood nineteen tenements, backing on to the garden of York House, which in Baker's time was occupied by the Lord Keeper, Sir Thomas Egerton, later Baron Ellesmere. The tenements had originally only had a depth of some twenty feet, but in 1596 the Archbishop of York had leased a strip of his garden to provide greater accommodation for the houses which backed on to it.[24]

Elizabeth Baker probably had a hand in the move to the Strand. Jane Jeames, the maidservant, recalled that 'his said first wife ye Flaxwoman . . . helped to gett him somethinge by her trade aforesaid'. To and fro along the Strand passed the ceaseless traffic between the Port of London, the Tower and the City to the east and the Palaces of Westminster, Whitehall and St James's to the west. Along the south side of the Strand stood another cluster of private palaces – the Savoy, Salisbury House, Durham House, York House and Hungerford House. Here in the Strand was the perfect site for a haberdasher who intended to supply expensive wares to rich fashion-loving customers. Here, with his wife's experience with flax in the making of linen to help him, Robert Baker (again in the words of Jane Jeames) 'fell after his being a Taylor . . . into a way of makinge Pickadillys and Kept many men att worke and gott a great deale of money by it'.[17]

Many other people told the same story. William Robinson, for instance, whose father-in-law had served at Tilbury in 1588, possibly with Baker, said that his 'first Risinge was his makeing of Pickadillys for most of the Nobilitie and Gentrie'. John Harris, gentleman, who had been born and bred in a house opposite the Seven Stars in the Strand, said that 'by ye meanes of ye Ladie Cope of Kensington, whose Taylor hee was, [Baker] fell to makeinge of Pickadillies and kept many men att worke in it'.[17]

Lady Cope was the wife of Sir Walter Cope, the builder of Cope Castle (later Holland House, Kensington), and had previously lived in the Strand; she may therefore have been one of Baker's first important customers.

Elizabeth Robinson said that 'hee kept about three score men att worke' in making 'Pickadillies' in the Strand. By this time the little tenement in York Rents had become a grossly overcrowded factory; an extension was urgently required. And now good fortune visited Robert Baker again, for Elizabeth Robinson also related that his 'first Rise was his findeinge a pott of money when hee built a back house in ye Strand behind the Seaven Starrs'; and this improbable evidence was supported by Elizabeth Andrews, who said that 'upon his building att the said house called the Seaven Starres in the Strand he found money which made him a gentleman as well as his makeinge pickadillies'.[17]

So within a few years of opening his shop in the Strand Robert Baker had become a man of substance. In 1608 he contributed twenty shillings to the repair of St Martin's Church. Next year he was one of the constables of the parish, and between 1609 and 1613 he was frequently a juryman at Quarter Sessions. He visited his relations in Taunton, where he was wined and dined by the principal citizens, for 'it was much talked of in the Towne of Taunton . . . what a great estate he had gotten' by the sale of pickadils.[15]

Between 1606 and 1612 his wife bore him six more children – two sons, John and Robert, and four daughters, Elizabeth, Judith, Sarah and Lucy – but all of them except Judith died in early childhood.[25]

In 1609 Robert Baker's trade must have been greatly helped by the redevelopment of the ground to the east of his shop. A range of ruinous stables which stood between Durham House and the street was bought by the Lord High Treasurer, Robert Cecil, Earl of Salisbury. On this site he erected 'a very goodly and beautiful building . . . after the fashion of the Royall Exchange in London'. Along the two-hundred-foot frontage to the street there was a covered arcade, behind which were ranged two rows of shops with a central gangway ten feet wide. There were three entrances from the Strand and at each end staircases led to more shops on the upper floor. In April 1609 James I and his Queen, Anne of Denmark, came 'with many great Lords, and chiefe Ladies' to open the building, 'and were there entertained with pleasant speeches, giftes, and ingenious devices, and then the King gave it a name, and called it Britaines Burse'.[26]

The shops were to be open from 6 a.m. to 8 p.m. in summer and from 7 a.m. to 7 p.m. in winter, and were only for the use of haberdashers, stocking-sellers, linen-drapers, seamsters, goldsmiths, jewellers, milliners, perfumers, silk mercers and similar tradesmen. To Britain's Burse came the rich fashion-conscious members of James's extravagant court; and next door stood Baker's pickadil shop.[26]

Three years later the royal extravagance provided Baker with another opportunity. After several abortive diplomatic flirtations James decided to marry his eldest daughter, the Lady Elizabeth, to Frederick, Count Palatine of the Rhine, whom he regarded as the probable future head of the Protestant interest in Germany. In May 1612 the marriage articles were drawn up, and in October Prince Frederick arrived in England to meet his bride.

James was determined to spare no expense – at their very first meeting he presented his future son-in-law with a ring valued at £1800. Feastings and pageants and merriments were provided on the most lavish scale. James and Queen Anne were charmed with the Prince, and the Prince, despite the diplomatic origin of the match, fell deeply in love with Lady Elizabeth. Even the tragic death in November of James's eldest son and heir, Prince Henry, only temporarily halted the rejoicings, and the death was a godsend to people in Baker's line of business, for at very short notice all the court had to buy mourning as well as wedding apparel. The betrothal ceremony took place at the Banqueting House in Whitehall Palace on 27 December. The Princess, 'to make an even mixture of joy and mourning, wore black satin with a little silver lace, and a plume of white feathers in her head, which fashion was taken up the next day of all the young gallants of the court and city, which hath made white feathers dear on the sudden.'[27]

The Lady Elizabeth's trousseau cost at least £10,000, and was provided on James's instructions by Lord Hay, Keeper of the Great Wardrobe, and Lord Harrington, Master of the Princess's Household. The accounts for this enormous expenditure survive in the Public Record Office, together with James's warrant to Lord Hay ordering him to 'laye out unto the persons hereafter named for all suche parcells of Stuf and workemanship by them don or delyverid or otherwise employed at the Marriadge of our deare Doughter the Lady Elizabeth'. Robert Grigge, John Hull and Thomas Wooderone, mercers, Benjamin Henshaw and Christopher Weaver, silkmen, John Spens, Edward Thomasen, and Thomas Watson, tailors, each supplied many hundreds of poundsworth of goods; a dozen other tradesmen supplied lesser quantities, and last came 'Robert Baker, Taylor, for Twelve collers of white satten, lyned with taphata, stitched with silke, and stiffenid; for silke, stiffenynge, and making six tyssued collors and embroidered Collers', £21 12s.[28]

After the betrothal ceremony there were more feastings, fêtes and exchanges of lavish presents. James dreaded the impending departure of his beloved daughter for Germany (she was only sixteen) and was reluctant to fix a day for the wedding. He saw as much as he could of her. Every evening he played cards with her at Whitehall – he always won, and Lord Harrington had to pay the King her debts, nearly twenty pounds spread over four weeks.[29] But at last the day was appointed, the masques, the fireworks and the mock naval fights on the river were over, and the ceremony took place in the chapel of Whitehall Palace on 14 February 1613. The King himself gave away the bride; she wore a dress of Florence cloth of silver, richly embroidered, and on her head a crown of gold, brilliantly decked with diamonds and pearls, from which pendants mingled with her long and beautiful hair, which drooped over her shoulders down to the waist. The Archbishop of Canterbury performed the nuptial ceremony, and afterwards there was a banquet, a masque and a ball.

After the wedding James found that the exchequer was bankrupt. Lord Harrington had to be satisfied for most of his expenses with the grant of the privilege of coining brass farthings, and the bridal couple were hustled off to Germany to prevent any more expense. James bade adieu to his daughter at Canterbury – he never saw her again – and returned home to pay the bills.

Robert Baker's recorded share in the supply of the trousseau only amounted to a comparatively small sum, but he may well have provided other items, for the accounts do not always specify the name of the supplier. The mere fact that he received even a small order on such an important occasion shows the standing to which he had now attained; and if he supplied 'embroidered Collers' to the value of £21 to royalty it may safely be surmised that he also supplied them on a much greater scale to James's guests and courtiers, whose combined total expenditure on wearing apparel in connexion with the wedding must have been prodigious. It was a far cry from the days when he had worked as a journeyman for Mr Brales at the Flying Horse.

2 *Robert Baker the Speculative Builder*

The wealth and prosperity which Robert Baker derived from the Lady Elizabeth's marriage enabled him to take the first step towards establishing himself as a landed gentleman – the dream of every successful tradesman in those days. What he needed was a house near his very over-crowded business premises in the Strand, and a few months before the royal wedding festivities he bought $1\frac{3}{8}$ acres of freehold ground in Windmill Field for £50 from the heirs of one John Golightly. This plot was then in the open country, about ten minutes' walk from the Seven Stars in the Strand. It was a narrow strip of land bounded on the south by the road to Colnbrook (now Coventry Street), and on the west by the track (now Great Windmill Street) leading to the windmill, which stood where Ham Yard is now. This ground was Lammas common land over which the parishioners of St Martin in the Fields had grazing rights from Lammas Day (12 August) until the spring. Baker intended to enclose and build on it, and so he had to recompense the parishioners for the loss of their rights over it. On 9 July 1612 the vestry of St Martin in the Fields imposed on him an annual payment of thirty shillings for the enclosure of this ground, whereon he and John Baker (probably a cousin) 'have builded certaine houses'.[1]

The decision to buy and build on this land was only taken after long consideration, for in 1658 Elizabeth Andrews remembered how Robert Baker used to come to her father's house 'and severall times asked . . . [him] whether hee the said Robert Baker had best to buy the said land, and did advise with her said late father to that purpose.' She also said that Baker's new house there 'was afterwards by Queen Anne . . . named or called Pickadilly'. As the bride's mother, Anne of Denmark probably knew all about her daughter Princess Elizabeth's trousseau, and who supplied it; so she may well have suggested the name. But Paul Bettering, who as a young man had worked with Baker and clubbed with 'other journeymen tailors that were Somersettshire men', also claimed (in very confused phraseology) to have been its author; he had been 'one that helped to name it soe, for hee diverse times told ye said Robert Baker, whoe besides his said trade of a Taylor free to makeinge of Pickadillies, that hee gott more by makeinge Pickadillys than by his Tayloring, and that therefore whyther that built as aforesaid should be called Pickadilly Hall'.[2] Whoever first suggested the name certainly did so soon after Baker's new house was built, for on 20 September 1614 the Westminster Court of Burgesses referred to it by name when they ordered one Hugh Parsons to cease selling beer and tobacco at a house 'near a place there called Pickadilly Hall'.[3]

17

There is no contemporary description of Piccadilly Hall. In his will Baker described it as 'the howse or messuage wherein I now dwell, with the garden and cowhouse to the same adioyninge', which does not suggest that it was large or pretentious.[4] It is also interesting that he did not refer to it as Piccadilly Hall, which may imply that he disliked the name as being a derisive reference to the source of his wealth. In 1651 a survey of all the buildings in the neighbourhood was made. The house occupied by Robert Baker's widow – presumably the original Piccadilly Hall – was then described as a 'Tenement strongly built with Bricks and covered with Tile, consisting [of] one Seller, one Hall, a Kitchen and a Larder below staires, and in the first story above staires 2 Chambers and a Closet there, and over the same 2 Garret roomes, which together with one Court yard, a Garden and a backside, conteyninge by estimacion 3 Roods'.[5] The house stood somewhere on the east side of Great Windmill Street to the south of Archer Street; the site may have corresponded roughly with that of the house erected in 1767 by Dr William Hunter, the façade of which still survives on the east side of Great Windmill Street as part of the Lyric Theatre.

Robert Baker had only lived at Piccadilly Hall for about two years when his wife Elizabeth, the flaxwoman, died, and was buried at St Martin in the Fields on 16 July 1614.[6] She remains a shadowy figure, working hard in the shop in the intervals between giving birth to numerous children, of whom only two, Frances, now aged twelve, and Judith, aged six, survived her.

Within thirteen months Baker had married again. His second bride was Mary Slye, a young widow whose first husband, Thomas Slye, had lived and died in the parish of St Mary Le Strand. Whether Mary brought any of her first husband's estate with her to her new home at Piccadilly Hall is not clear, but there is some reason to think that Baker may have married her for her fortune, and she may very well have married *him* for *his* money, for she was quite able to look after herself. The wedding took place at St Martin in the Fields on 15 August 1615.[7]

The principal figure in the family into which Baker had now married was his new father-in-law, Stephen Higgins, the formidable apothecary who lived in the Liberty of the Savoy. In 1603 Higgins had served as a constable there, and his name was even suggested – by someone who evidently knew little about him – as a suitable person to be made a Justice of the Peace. Ten years later he was admitted to the livery of the Grocers' Company, to which apothecaries then belonged, but he refused to play the customary part in the company's social activities. In 1617, when the Society of Apothecaries was founded, he had attained sufficient eminence in his practice of medicine to be named as one of the two original wardens of the new body. In 1621 and again in 1638 he served as master of the society, but in between whiles he was quarrelling with his professional colleagues. They described him as 'an obstinate, contentious and troublesome person', and in 1631 he even suffered partial expulsion from the society.[8]

Higgins had other irons in the fire besides medicine, for like his son-in-law Baker he was interested in real property and in the money which could by unscrupulous means be made from it in the disorderly suburbs of early seventeenth-century London. The

Government had been much concerned by the problems posed by these new suburbs, and since 1580 had attempted to ban the outward expansion of London.[9] In a proclamation issued in that year Queen Elizabeth did 'charge and straightly command all manner of Persons, of what qualitie soever they be, to desist and forbeare from any new buildings of any house or tenement within three miles from any of the gates of the said citie of London'. This was the policy of the Green Belt, which was unavailingly continued, with some modification of detail, in a long series of proclamations issued by James I, Charles I, Cromwell and Charles II until it was finally abandoned in the 1670s, shortly after the Great Fire. By this time the complete prohibition on building had long been abandoned in favour of limitation by the sale of licences to build, and the failure of the ban was plain for all to see in the new streets of Holborn, Covent Garden, Lincoln's Inn and many other new suburban areas. London had proved too strong to be hemmed in, and until the idea of a Green Belt was revived (for quite different reasons) in the 1920s, neither the Government nor the municipal authorities made any attempt to limit its incessant expansion again.

Fear of disorder, famine and plague – or, as Lord Treasurer Burghley described it, 'Reservation of Her Majesty's Person, Sustentation of her Subjects with victuals, preservation from the Plague' – were the motives for the Tudor Green Belt. Not more than one family was to inhabit any house, and lodgers were to depart forthwith. In 1593 an Act of Parliament reinforced the proclamation, and 'many and spetiall directions' were sent in the Queen's name to the Lord Mayor and the Justices of the Peace for Middlesex to enforce the regulations. Elizabeth raged at the Justices' 'slacke and negligent oversight' and in 1602 she issued another proclamation. Within the three-mile radius there was to be no new building, no sub-division of existing houses, shacks erected within the last seven years were to be demolished, and offenders were to be summoned before the Court of Star Chamber. But still 'contemptious persons' continued to build; stables were converted into houses, inconspicuous gardens and courts were covered with jerry-built sheds, and even prefabrication was often practised, for some of 'those that doe make newe buildings doe cause the frame to be made in other places and suddenly sett upp the same'.

The attempt to curb the growth of London defeated its own ends, for it aggravated over-crowding, particularly in the suburbs where control was looser than in the City itself, and so increased the risk of disorder and the spread of plague. In 1603, when James I came down from Scotland with his motley crowd of impecunious fellow-countrymen to take possession of his new kingdom, 30,000 Londoners are said to have died of the plague. By September James had ingloriously retreated to Woodstock, whence he issued a proclamation in which he admitted that 'the number of dissolute and idle persons, and the pestering of many of them in small and strait rooms hath been a great cause of the plague'. But soon he was re-iterating the old policy, in characteristically ambiguous terms; no new house was to be built before Michaelmas 1605, and thereafter no new house was to be built within a mile of the suburbs unless the walls and windows were made of brick or stone.

This proved no more effective than the earlier pronouncements, and so in November 1607 James, 'perceiving the great inconveniences which dayly doe arise', issued another more drastic proclamation. By this time the King had also perceived that the incessant expansion of London could be used as a source of revenue, and this proclamation therefore contained the important innovation that no new houses were to be built in or about the capital except by special licence. There were also a number of other detailed regulations which formed a microcosm of modern planning practice. There was to be no new building within two miles of any of the gates of the City of London except on old foundations or in the courtyard of a house – in-filling in the Green Belt was permissible. Unlicensed sheds and shops built within the previous five years were to be pulled down – today the maximum period for dealing with such offences is four years. There was to be no unauthorised change of use, for cellars erected within the last five years were not 'to be used for lodgings, or tipling or victualling houses', and there was to be strict control of the elevations of new houses built on old foundations, which were to be built in a uniform style to be approved by the aldermen of the City. There was to be no further sub-division of tenements, but additions could be made to existing buildings provided that they did not exceed one third of the area of the old structure. The whole of this complicated code was to be administered by the seventeenth-century equivalent of local council and Whitehall ministry – the aldermen of the City, the Justices of the Peace and the Court of Star Chamber.

By the summer of 1608 James was receiving a useful little income from fines imposed upon offenders in the Star Chamber, but he was also complaining at the neglect of his officers. The whole system was, of course, quite unworkable as well as being irrelevant to its avowed objects, the prevention of plague, famine and disorder. The vast administrative machine required to administer modern planning policy did not exist in the seventeenth century, James was frequently modifying his regulations – two more proclamations were issued in 1611 – and he had not made up his mind whether he really wanted to stop building or to get money out of licences and fines. The suburbs of London had, in fact, become a building speculator's dream.

In the exploitation of this situation Stephen Higgins specialised in small-scale hole-and-corner activities such as buying up stables and surreptitiously converting them into tenements. In 1611, for instance, he was in trouble with the Westminster Court of Burgesses about 'the building of an House in Drewry Lane which was sometime a Stable', and then his tenant introduced lodgers into the house, contrary to the proclamations, and fathered an illegitimate child there. Higgins successfully ignored the repeated orders of the Court to appear and fix a day 'for the converting of his Tenement into a Stable again', and started building in the Liberty of the Savoy. Here he was soon involved with his neighbours in a dispute about ancient lights, and being a hardened old sinner he had the effrontery to take the matter to the Court of Star Chamber. The indignant neighbours replied that Higgins was 'a man of verie naughtie disposition, . . . transported with heate of rage and furie', and started a counter-offensive at Middlesex Sessions. Here Higgins was peremptorily ordered to produce the building licence from

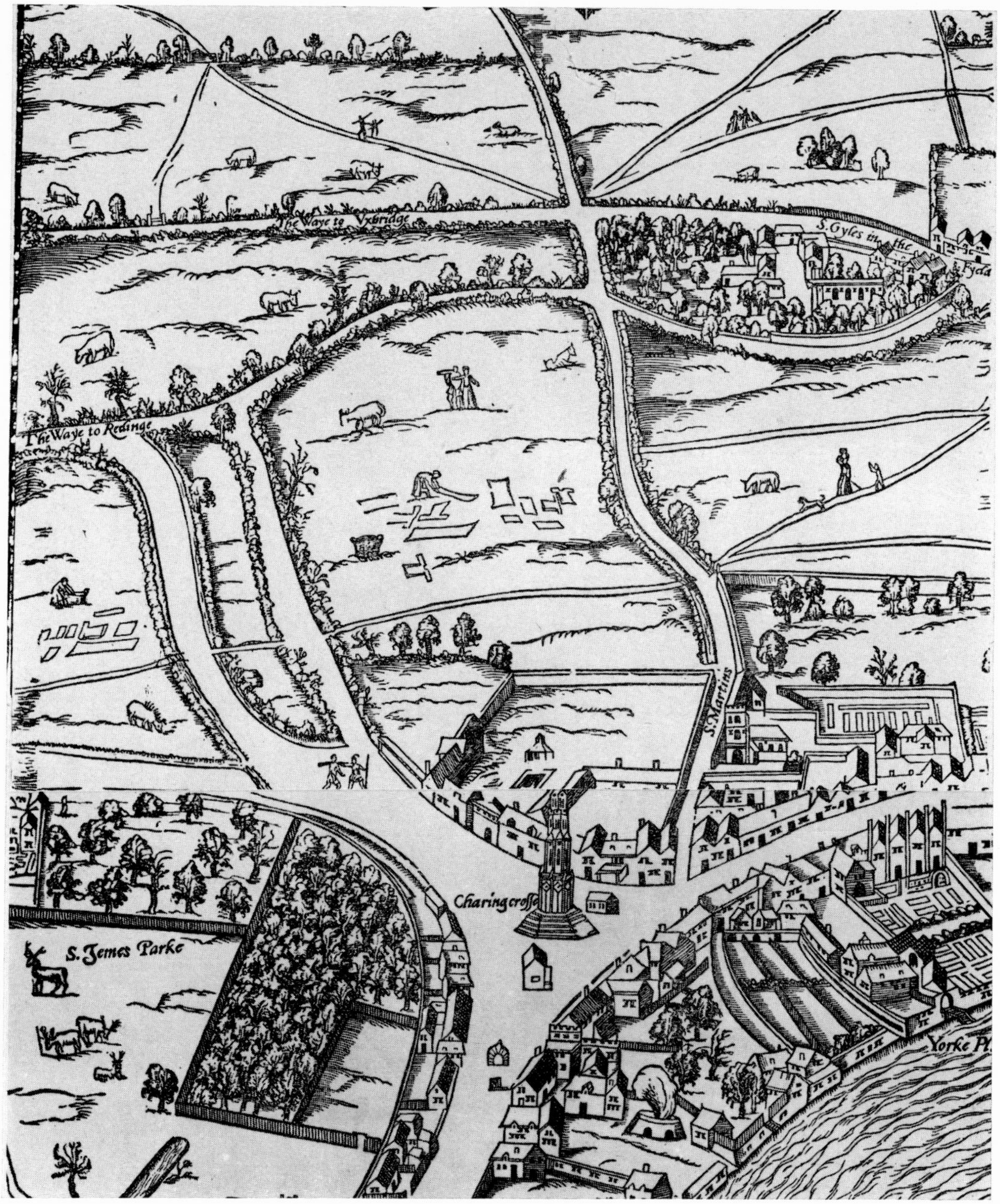
The Waye to Vxbridge
S. Gyles in the Fyld
The Waye to Redinge
S. Martins
Charingcrosse
S. Jemes Parke
Yorke Pl

Plate 1. Extract from the map attributed to Ralph Agas showing the Charing Cross, Piccadilly and Soho areas as in the 1550s

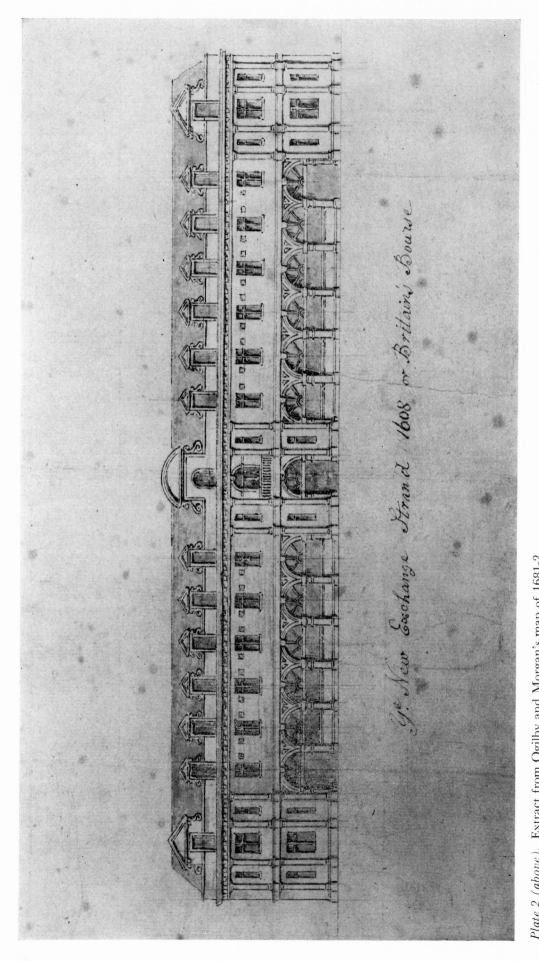

Ye New Exchange Strand 1608 or Britain's Bourse

Plate 2 (above). Extract from Ogilby and Morgan's map of 1681-2
Plate 3 (below). The New Exchange, or Britain's Bourse, Strand. *From a drawing in the Greater London Council Print Collection*

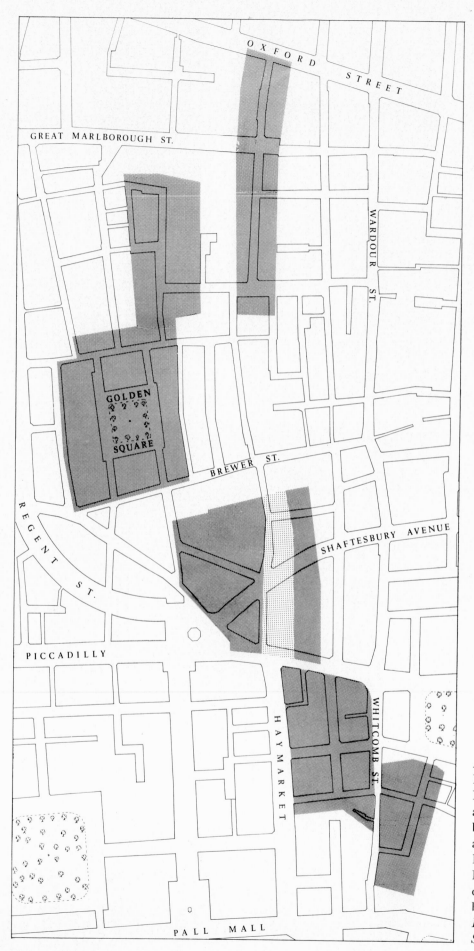

OXFORD STREET

GREAT MARLBOROUGH ST.

WARDOUR ST.

GOLDEN SQUARE

BREWER ST.

REGENT ST.

SHAFTESBURY AVENUE

PICCADILLY

HAYMARKET

WHITCOMB ST.

PALL MALL

Plate 4. Robert Baker's estate. Lightly hatched area denotes land bought in *c*1612 and the curtilage of Piccadilly Hall. Heavy hatching denotes the land bought in 1619. *Drawing by John Sambrook*

the Privy Council which he claimed to possess, and he apparently did so, for he was discharged. Three years later one of his neighbours in the Savoy started making additions to his house at the expense of Higgins's ancient lights, and Higgins told the Manor Court of the Duchy of Lancaster that he 'findes himself much agreeved'. But by this time – about 1620 – retribution was not far off, for in 1619 the Commissioners for Building (whom James had established in 1615 to cope with the suburbs of London) had required him to compound by a fine for his offences in both Drury Lane and the Savoy. At first he 'obstinately refused', but then the Privy Council, to whom the matter had been reported, ordered the Sheriffs of London and Middlesex to demolish all his buildings. How he reacted to this threat is not recorded, but one may guess that he submitted and paid up.[10]

Robert Baker's speculative activities were generally rather different. Unlike his new father-in-law, he was not in constant trouble with the authorities, and his respectable career in petty public office continued. After serving as a constable and juryman he was appointed an overseer of the poor in 1614 and two years later he was a sidesman. The worst that was ever said of him was that he was 'a man of a covetous dispocion',[11] which, when said (as in this case) by a prosecuting solicitor, may merely mean that in money matters he steered close to the wind. The parish accounts certainly support this view, for when, as overseer of the poor, it was his duty to collect the parish poor rates, he did not hesitate to enter his own name as paying nothing.

Unlike Higgins, Baker was astute enough to see that the outward expansion of London was going to continue, and that the value of land just outside the suburbs would in course of time increase prodigiously. The purpose of his first small investment in freehold land was not merely to obtain a site for a house for himself, but also to build other houses there. By 1617 he had built three houses as well as his own Piccadilly Hall on his ground on the east side of what is now Great Windmill Street, and by 1626 there were three more. The existence of these houses was never challenged by the authorities in Baker's life-time; they stood conspicuous and isolated in open country within a quarter of a mile of Whitehall, and it is therefore almost certain that he had obtained a building licence for them from the Privy Council. No record of such a licence has been found, but the registers of the Privy Council, where the licence would have been entered, are no longer extant for the years 1602 to 1613.[3]

While these apparently legal activities were proceeding at Piccadilly there were also more clandestine goings-on in the Strand, not unlike those of Stephen Higgins in the Savoy. Here in 1615 Baker obtained from the Archbishop of York a twenty-one-year lease of four houses near Britain's Burse, and shortly afterwards he started to make alterations and additions. In 1622 he was prosecuted by the attorney general at the Court of Star Chamber for having infringed the building proclamation of 1619. According to the attorney general he had rebuilt the fronts of the four houses in timber 'with great out juttyeing Cant Windows'. Baker replied that one of the houses, over four storeys high, had had a large garden at the back which he had intended to divide, 'alotting to the said houses a fitting portion, to the end that he might get better terms

for them all'. But the chimneystack of the principal house had fallen down and dam-
aged the other houses. He had repaired the chimney and divided up the garden, using
old materials as far as possible. He admitted setting out two windows, but claimed that
this was merely restoration of the windows that had existed there before. In any case,
the work had been completed before the proclamation of 12 March 1619 which had
contained fresh regulations about projecting windows. The decision of the Court is not
known, but no doubt Baker made a profit out of the houses.[11]

Baker's last and greatest speculation was concerned with freehold land. In the 1530s
Henry VIII had acquired large tracts of the land to the north and west of Whitehall
from which the water supply of the palace was obtained. Most of these lands had previously belonged to the Abbeys of Westminster and of Abingdon, Eton College, the
Mercers' Company and the Hospital of Burton Saint Lazar, and were intermingled one
with another. For some unexplained reason Queen Elizabeth had sold some sixty acres
of these lands, which had until the 1530s belonged to the Mercers' Company, and after
several rapid changes of ownership they were bought in 1561 by a prosperous brewer,
Thomas Wilson of St Botolph without Aldgate. He built the windmill from which
Great Windmill Street takes its name, and at his death in 1590 bequeathed his lands
to his son Richard. In January 1619 the latter sold twenty-two of his sixty acres to
Robert Baker. Years later his widow Mary claimed that she had provided him with
most of the purchase money.[12]

The value of these lands could be expected to increase enormously as the westward
growth of the suburbs proceeded. Nearest to London was a two-acre close, known as
the Blue Mews, situated on the east side of Whitcomb Street and to the south of Leicester Square. Shortly before his death Baker enclosed this land with a brick wall and
started building houses here.[4] A little to the west was Scavengers' Close, comprising the
land bounded by the Haymarket, Coventry Street, Wardour Street and the backs of
the houses on the south side of Orange Street. North of this was a substantial area on
the west side of Great Windmill Street, and a thin strip to the east of his first little
purchase on the east side of this street. North again was the largest piece, now occupied
by Golden Square, Marshall Street and the adjacent streets, and lastly there was the
long narrow strip extending as far north as Oxford Street, along which Poland Street
was later built. With the exception of the Marshall Street area, where the presence of
a pest house postponed building development until the 1730s, all of Baker's lands were
covered with streets and houses within some seventy years of his death.

After this great scoop Baker ceased to style himself tailor and became 'gentleman'.
Many years later one of his servants remembered him as 'livinge as a gentleman upon
his meanes at Pickadilly',[2] and one of his cousins, Emanuel Mico, a Taunton clothier,
who 'diverse times did meete and drinke with the said Robert Baker in the Cities of
London and Westminster', provided a physical description of him in these last years of
his life – he was 'of a middle stature, a good complexion and of a browne hayre mixed
with some gray haires'.[13]

In 1616 Baker's second wife had borne him a daughter, named Mary after her mother. He now had three daughters, and must have longed for a son and heir. He had to wait another four years, until 1620, for the fulfilment of his hopes. This son was named Robert, and in 1622 another was born and named Samuel.[14] By this time Frances Baker, his eldest surviving daughter by his first wife, was aged twenty, and the problem of arranging a suitable marriage for her had arisen. Robert Baker was now well able to provide her with a large enough dowry to attract the interest of the landed gentry, and in 1622 a marriage was arranged with Edward Hubert or Hobart, esquire, of Birchanger, Stansted, Essex. Hubert's grandfather, a successful lawyer who had been one of the six Clerks in Chancery, had bought an estate at Birchanger in 1584; his son, Sir Francis Hubert of Stansted Hall, had twelve children, of whom Edward was the eldest boy. At the time of his betrothal to Frances Baker, Edward Hubert was a young lawyer, recently admitted to Gray's Inn.

The provision of a suitable dowry for Frances formed part of a general settlement by which on 1 December 1622 Robert Baker arranged for the disposal of his estate amongst his wife, two sons and three daughters. This deed has not survived, but Frances's dowry consisted of five hundred pounds, plus (perhaps) the residue of the whole estate if all Robert's other children should die without issue. At this particular time Baker was evidently short of ready cash and unable to pay the five hundred pounds; he therefore signed a bond to pay Edward Hubert this sum plus interest by January 1624. Hubert was satisfied with this security and the marriage took place on 10 December 1622.[15]

Four months later Robert Baker died at Piccadilly Hall. In the will which he made a few hours before his death he described himself as gentleman of the parish of St Martin in the Fields, 'sicke in bodye but of perfect minde, thankes be to God'. 'First and principallie', he began, 'I commend and committ my Soule unto the handes of Almightie God, my Creator, hopinge of eternall Salvation through the merritts of my Saviour Jesus Christ that died for me and by no other meanes. Item as for my wordly estate, I devise the same as followeth . . .' The original copy of the will has not survived, so it is not known whether he was now able to sign his full name.[4] He was buried, not in the common graveyard, but within the church of St Martin in the Fields, by night, on 16 April 1623. The funeral dues amounted to £3 10s. 3d., the highest paid in the whole of that year.[16]

3 *Mary Baker's Inheritance*

Robert Baker died a very rich man. His freehold lands alone were worth two hundred pounds a year, and he also owned leasehold property in the Strand, as well as household effects and possibly some ready cash. As he struggled at Piccadilly Hall to make his will he may have been consoled with the sure knowledge that the value of his estate would almost automatically increase enormously with the expansion of London. He had travelled far since the days when he had 'wrought with one Mr. Tankynes, a Taylor in Taunton, as a journeyman'. He had made his fortune, and now in his death agony he was bequeathing to his family a London estate that would soon be comparable in value with those of the Cecils in St Martin's Lane or of the Russells in Covent Garden – two of the greatest families in England.

But he bequeathed no happiness, and all his efforts to establish the Bakers of Somerset as landed gentry came to nothing. Through no fault of his he left bitterness, strife and misery, and his life-time's labour produced nothing but greed, trickery, envy and hatred. Family quarrels over money are always degrading. The links of kinship are too strong to permit escape from them, and when they extend over a whole life-span, as they often do, they gnaw away the very vitals of human love and charity. For the Bakers, as for many others, life might have been better if they had never had a wealthy forebear and Robert had remained as a journeyman with Mr Tankynes in Taunton, poor.

The problem of settling the estate was extremely difficult. At the time of his death Robert Baker had five living children – Frances and Judith, daughters of his first wife, and Mary, Robert and Samuel, the children of his second wife, who was then pregnant again. He had already provided for Frances at the time of her marriage with Edward Hubert (although her portion had not been fully paid), but all the others were still under age, Judith, the eldest, being only fifteen. The whole problem was complicated by his evident omission to provide his second wife Mary with any jointure, although he had intended to do so;[1] and finally he had to take into account the fact that the Crown, acting through the Court of Wards, would have certain rights over the estate during the long minority of his heir.

First of all he appointed a cousin, Samuel Baker, whom he described as of the parish of St Clement Danes, gentleman, as his sole executor. (As events turned out, he would have been wiser to have appointed more than one executor.) Samuel Baker was instructed to sell all the leasehold property not specifically mentioned elsewhere in the

24

will, and from the proceeds Edward Hubert was to be paid the marriage portion which should have been paid at the time of his marriage with Frances Baker. Samuel Baker was also to pay himself fifty pounds in settlement of a debt which Robert Baker owed him, and another fifty pounds to Mr Bale, possibly the Mr Brales of the Flying Horse in the Strand. The widow Mary Baker was to have Piccadilly Hall and the two houses in the Strand for her life, her younger son Samuel was to have the two acres of the Blue Mews to the south of Leicester Square, plus the two houses in the Strand after his mother's death, and the unborn child was to have Scavengers' Close, to the east of the Haymarket, and, after his mother's death, Piccadilly Hall. All the rest of the freehold estate was of course to descend to the elder son, Robert, who when his father died was not quite three years old.

Samuel Baker the executor was to administer the income of the freehold estate for twelve years after the testator's death. He was to pay to whoever should 'have the education and bringing upp' of the two boys, Robert and Samuel, twenty pounds each a year, and the same amount for the daughter Mary. The rest of the income was to be allowed to accumulate, and when Judith and Mary married or came of age they were to receive six hundred pounds each as their marriage portion.

As a reward for his projected twelve years of 'paines to be taken about the mannidginge of the business concerninge this will' Samuel Baker the executor was bequeathed the sum of four pounds 'to buy him a Ringe'. The only charitable bequest was the conventional one to the poor of the parish of St Martin in the Fields, who received fifty shillings and ten shillings' worth of bread.[1]

The purpose of this will was to provide for all the family and establish the elder son, Robert, with a valuable freehold estate. The subsequent history of the Bakers of Piccadilly provides a text-book illustration of Burns's sad remark that

> The best laid schemes o' mice an' men
> Gang aft a-gley.

Death came very quickly, for the child which Mary Baker was carrying was evidently still-born, and within three months of Robert Baker's death his younger son, Samuel, only one year old, also died,[2] and his share of the estate passed to his elder brother. A few weeks later Samuel Baker the executor found that the widow Mary Baker would not co-operate with him in the administration of the will. All the leases and title deeds of the estate were kept at Piccadilly Hall, where she and her brood of young children were still living, and she refused to hand them over to the executor. She was supported by her father, Stephen Higgins the apothecary, and although Samuel Baker 'often entreated' them, they put him off with fair promises. But there was no time to delay, for Samuel Baker was now responsible for carrying out Robert Baker's obligation to pay Edward Hubert the five hundred pounds plus interest due to him for the marriage portion of his wife Frances; and if this sum was not paid by January 1624, the debt due to Hubert would be doubled. By November 1623 time was getting short and as the widow Baker and her father, who must have known the position perfectly well, remained evasive, Samuel Baker started a suit in the Court of Chancery to compel them to hand over the deeds.[3] But before the Court could do anything Samuel Baker the executor died, in February 1624.[4]

Mary Baker was still a young woman, but she had been twice widowed, had lost one fortune, and was therefore determined to make the best of her claims to the Baker estate. Her first husband, Thomas Slye, had inherited lands in five counties from his father, but as he was not of age his estate had come within the jurisdiction of the Court of Wards. On his death, still in his minority, the estate had passed to his younger brother, William Slye, subject to his young widow's rightful claim for dower. This claim had been recognised by the Court of Wards, and entitled Mary to a life interest in one third of the properties. But the division of such a scattered estate took time, and before it had been completed William Slye had also died, leaving his two elder sisters as his co-heiresses. The Slye family trustee had then gained possession of the legal papers, and all Mary Baker's efforts – for by this time she had remarried – to obtain her share had been ignored. In the Court of Wards she was met with the plea that as the Slye sisters were of age the Court no longer had any jurisdiction over the estate, and she had no more success either at common law or in Chancery.[5]

It is therefore easy to understand why, after the death of her second husband, Robert Baker, she was determined to keep possession of the title deeds of the estate. Moreover Robert Baker had intended that his bequests to her of Piccadilly Hall and the two houses in the Strand should be a substitute for her right of dower to one third of the income of the whole estate for the remainder of her life. The will had specifically stated that these bequests were 'to my lovinge wife Marye in lieue and recompence of her dower'.[1] One third of the income of the whole estate was worth far more than the revenue from the bequests, and so Mary Baker decided to disregard her husband's intentions and claim her dower.

The death of Samuel Baker the executor in February 1624 greatly strengthened Mary Baker's position. The administration of Robert Baker's will passed to Mr Gregory Baker of the Castle of Windsor, gentleman, who was presumably a relative of Samuel's, although only referred to as a 'good friend'. Until his death thirteen years later Gregory Baker kept accounts 'about the business of Robert Baker of Pickadillie', and paid out money for the maintenance of the children, but he seems to have allowed Mary Baker and her father Stephen Higgins a free hand in the crucial matter of dealing with the Court of Wards.[6]

The Crown had rights of wardship over the whole of Robert Baker's freehold property because a small part of it, including the site of Piccadilly Hall, was held by knight service in chief from the King. During the minority of an heir the knight service could not be performed – so ran the theory – and the King therefore had the right to the custody of the estate and the bestowal of the ward in marriage. In practice these rights were sold, very often to a close relative of the ward, and as active knight service in time of war was no longer demanded in the seventeenth century, the ancient feudal idea of land tenure by military service had been converted into a source of Crown revenue.

In the spring of 1626 the Crown's rights to the wardship and marriage of Robert Baker the son were sold to his grandfather, Stephen Higgins, and his mother, Mary Baker, for £66 13s. 4d.[7] This was a perfectly normal way of disposing of a wardship, although Robert Baker the father had probably intended that his executor, Samuel Baker, now dead, should buy the rights, rather than the avaricious old apothecary Higgins. At about the same time Mary Baker refused to accept the bequests to her contained in the will, and was awarded the widow's usual dower of one third of the estate instead.[8]

But these well-laid schemes, by which Higgins had a free hand to engage in building operations, also went a-gley, for in 1628 the ward, Robert Baker, died at the age of seven. He was the last surviving son, so the estate passed to his sister, Mary, who was then aged twelve, and in due course her mother, the widow Mary Baker, bought the rights of wardship again for forty pounds.[7] Higgins resumed effective control once more.

Higgins was a speculator, and within a short while he had persuaded his daughter, the widow, to lease the ground at the east corner of Coventry Street and the Haymarket to Simon Osbaldeston for building. Osbaldeston was the Lord Chamberlain's gentleman barber, and was therefore well placed to ignore or evade the regulations against building. Precisely how he did this is, of course, not recorded, but by 1636 he had laid out gardens and built a gaming house there, which was at once nicknamed Shaver's Hall in the same allusive manner as Robert Baker's house had previously been nicknamed Piccadilly Hall. Soon it became a favourite resort for members of the court at Whitehall, and the stakes were sometimes very high.

The commissioners who administered the building regulations were not likely to question a fashionable establishment like Shaver's Hall, but Mary Baker had granted other leases in the vicinity of Piccadilly. Less imposing houses had been built and in 1636 there had been a severe outbreak of plague in London, during which she and the occupants of several other of her houses at Piccadilly had been infected and shut up for four weeks with a guard set before their doors to prevent their coming out. This greatly alarmed the authorities, for the conduits which brought water to Whitehall and Somerset House extended across the Baker lands. So the Court of Star Chamber issued peremptory orders that 'all the Houses about Piccadilly' should be demolished forthwith,[9] and an enormous fine of one thousand pounds was imposed on Mrs Baker for 'continuing buildings unlawfully erected to the annoyance and putrefaction of his Majesty's springs of water'.[10]

Widow Baker proved quite capable of dealing with this catastrophe. She offered to build a brick conduit for the upper reaches of the stream, and to convey the water from a point above her houses to the palace in lead pipes, all of which she would pay for herself.[11] In May 1638 the Privy Council debated this plea and referred it to Inigo Jones, the Surveyor of the Works, for a report on its feasibility.[12] He considered that it was possible, and within a year Mrs Baker had laid the lead pipes and a 'great Dreyne for the bringing the Water', and built a conduit head, at a total cost of six hundred pounds. But according to Inigo Jones there were still two great ponds near Piccadilly which were used 'to wash diseased Horses and Doggs in', and these, he insisted, must be filled up and proper soak-aways constructed. The Privy Council ordered that these works should be completed at once, and in November 1639, after Inigo Jones had certified that the waters were now being 'conveyed sweet and serviceable for his Majesty's use', the Council agreed to cancel the order to demolish all the houses at Piccadilly, and to consider the mitigation of the fine.[13]

In her dealings with the Privy Council Widow Baker had a new ally. In August 1636 her only surviving child, Mary, then aged twenty and heiress to the whole of Robert Baker's estate, subject only to her mother's life interest, by right of dower, to one third of the income, had married Henry Oxenden. The Oxendens had flourished for centuries in Kent. The family mansion at Dean, some six miles from Canterbury, had been rebuilt during the reign of Queen Elizabeth, and here Sir James Oxenden lived with his large family. Henry, his eldest son, had travelled for his education, or possibly served with the army abroad, and later had engaged in business of some kind in London with his father. But first and foremost Henry was a countryman, busying himself in Kentish affairs and the management of the family lands. At the time of his marriage he was aged twenty-two. A portrait shows a narrow sensitive, almost melancholy face, and long dark hair curling down over his shoulders.[14]

A few months after the marriage Henry Oxenden and Widow Baker agreed to divide the estate. She was to keep the lands and houses round Piccadilly, including the site of Osbaldeston's gaming house, and comprising about one third of the whole estate, for the rest of her life, and Oxenden and his wife Mary were to have the rest, plus Widow Baker's third after her death.[15] Henry Oxenden's father, Sir James, acted as trustee for the settlement, and in order to safeguard it Sir James guaranteed to the Privy Council that Widow Baker would execute the expensive piping and drainage works required at Piccadilly.[11]

In the normal course of events the Oxendens might now have enjoyed the great wealth of Robert Baker's estate for all time. But once again events did not turn out as everyone hoped and intended. In November 1638 Henry Oxenden's young wife gave birth to a daughter, but died eight days later. Once again the estate was back in the Court of Wards, and once again Widow Baker purchased the rights of wardship, in association with her aged father Stephen Higgins and her brother, Arnold Higgins. On this occasion she had to pay three hundred pounds – more than three times as much as before, for the value of the estate had already greatly increased – and as she had just paid six hundred pounds for the Piccadilly waterworks and was therefore short of cash she was allowed eighteen months in which to pay the full sum.[8]

Henry Oxenden does not seem to have grieved long over the death of his wife, for there is no reference in his letters to either his dead wife or his infant daughter. Perhaps he had only married Miss Baker for her money and now that she had failed to provide him with a son to inherit the estate he wanted to forget the whole episode. At all events he quickly married again and had a large family, and only his first wife's daughter, another Mary, remained to keep alive the memory of his short-lived first marriage. When her grandmother, the Widow Baker, and her father, Henry Oxenden, were both dead, Mary Oxenden would inherit the whole of Robert Baker's wealth, and lucky would be the man whom she married.

But of course this never happened, for when she was only eight or nine years old she died.[15] There is no reference to her death in her father's correspondence. Financially, he gained by the death of his daughter. The revenues from two-thirds of the Baker estate which Widow Baker had received as the purchaser of Mary Oxenden's wardship now reverted to Henry Oxenden for the rest of his life, and when Widow Baker died – as surely she must soon – he would receive the remaining third too. What happened after his death was no concern of his – or so he must have thought.

Who, indeed, would be the right heir, now that all Widow Baker's children, and her only grandchild, were dead? The strongest candidate, one might suppose, was Frances Hubert, the elder of Robert Baker's two daughters by his first wife, the flaxwoman in the Strand. She had married Edward Hubert, the lawyer of Gray's Inn, in 1622, and her father had engaged to provide her with a marriage portion of five or six hundred pounds. When he died a few months later this sum was still unpaid, but his executor was required to settle the matter at once. Frances was the only one of Robert Baker's numerous daughters who survived the triple hazards of infancy, childhood and child-bearing and reached middle age. She and her husband lived at Gifford's Buildings in St Giles in the Fields, Holborn, near the inns of court, where she bore at least one son, another Edward, who reached manhood. In this household also lived Frances' younger sister, Judith Baker, who died, unmarried, in 1633, aged twenty-four. Sadly she had recorded in her will that she had not received the marriage portion of six hundred pounds which her father Robert Baker had intended for her. She nominated her brother-in-law, Edward Hubert, as her executor, and bequeathed him four hundred pounds, if her portion were ever paid. All her wearing apparel was to go to her sister, Frances, and there was ten shillings for a mourning ring for her half-sister Mary Baker, who lived with the Widow Baker at Piccadilly Hall.[16]

The Huberts were the first of the contenders for the inheritance of the Baker estate. They maintained their claim in the Court of Chancery for over thirty years. Sometimes they were importunate, at other times they kept mum, listening and waiting for long periods while rival claimants argued and bickered with each other. But always they were hovering near-by, on the outskirts of the main battle, hoping to pick up some lucky windfall.

The Huberts' campaign was opened shortly after the death of little Mary Oxenden in about 1646. For some years it was directed against Widow Baker only, Henry Oxenden's life interest in two thirds of the estate being unchallenged. At first they tried, rather unwisely, to trick her. They alleged that 'during those troublesome tymes' when she had had to spend large sums on pipes and drains in order to prevent her houses being demolished, they had helped her by lending her one hundred pounds. She had not repaid them – so they claimed – and they had therefore started proceedings to obtain judgment for possession of her lands. To all this the widow replied that she had paid interest on the loan and had offered to return the principal too, but the Huberts were merely 'thirsting after the possession of the said lands and Tenements' and had therefore refused to accept her proffered repayment. In due course the dispute wound its tortuous way from the Petty Bag Office through the King's Bench to the Court of Chancery, and there, as so often happened, it petered out.[17]

Frances Hubert, the last of Robert Baker's children, died in about 1652. Her claim devolved upon her son Edward, who was now of age and described as of Much (i.e. Great) Baddow, Essex, gentleman. He soon resumed the attack with a petition in Chancery, but no longer maintained that the loan was unpaid. He now made the much more damaging claim that Robert Baker in his life-time had settled part of his estate on his wife Mary as her jointure; after his death she had deliberately concealed this settlement and so been able to obtain possession for life of one third of the estate by right of dower. Widow Baker, he asserted, 'doth hold both Jointure and dower', and had been able to do so through keeping possession of all the deeds of her husband's estate. He therefore prayed the Court to compel her to produce the documents of title for examination.[18]

Widow Baker made Edward Hubert wait for nearly a year for her answer to his petition. Finally she put in her rejoinder and when the case was heard in February 1656 'in the presence of the Councell learned on both sides' she was able to show that his petition was mistaken; Hubert was ordered to pay her costs.[19]

By this time, however, the two principal claimants were engaging lawyers, collecting evidence and preparing bills of complaint. News of Robert Baker's doings 'att London', and of the death of most of his children, had filtered down to the taverns of Taunton, where the family's fortunes were much discussed. Robert Baker's elder brother, the Taunton mercer, had had two sons, William and John. They had gone to live at Wellington, six miles south-west of Taunton, where they worked for John Hayne, a shoemaker, as servants or journeymen. Two of the sons of Alexander Bull, 'usher of the free schoole at Taunton', were also shoemakers in Wellington, and at least one of them was a journeyman employed by John Hayne. One day shortly after the death of Henry Oxenden's daughter, Mary, Alexander Bull went to Wellington to visit his sons. There he also saw William and John Baker, and knowing all the latest news about their family in London he 'acquainted the said William Baker that the said Robert Baker of Pickadilly, his uncle, and all or most of his children beinge then dead, the Lands of the said Robert Baker of Pickadilly might probably discend and come unto him the said William Baker of Wellington as next heire to the said Robert Baker'. And being a schoolmaster, and therefore much respected for his sagacity, he went on to advise the bewildered William 'to exhibit his bill in Chancery for examinacion of witnesses to preserve theire testimonyes while he the said Alexander Bull and others were living who knew the Pedigree of him the said William Baker'.[20]

William and John had always hoped that they might benefit from their uncle's prosperity – years ago they had even visited him at Piccadilly Hall – but now that death had removed most of the prior claimants they suddenly found themselves in the running for enormous wealth. But how could two poor ignorant Somerset shoemakers obtain recognition of their rights? They had no idea, and soon after Alexander Bull had delivered his agitating news they both died.[21]

So the claim passed to William Baker's elder son, John Baker, who was Robert Baker's great nephew. To match his pretensions he gave up shoemaking and described himself as 'gentleman'; he employed lawyers to promote his affairs and probably he went to London to establish himself in person as heir to the whole estate after the deaths of Widow Baker and Henry Oxenden. According to his own version he was for some fifteen years recognised as such by them, and he even joined with Oxenden in granting leases. For fifteen years he, a poor shoemaker's son, enjoyed the prospect of great wealth; and then suddenly a formidable rival appeared, who asserted that John Baker was an imposter and that he, James Baker, yeoman, of Evercreech in Somerset, was Robert Baker's great-nephew and right heir.

4 *The Court of Chancery*

In 1653 it was said that there were twenty-three thousand causes depending in the Court of Chancery. Some of them had been there for over thirty years, and scores of thousands of pounds had been spent, to the 'utter undoing of many families'. So Praise-God-Barebones' Parliament gaily voted for the abolition of the Court; the unholy muddle of the law was to be condensed 'into the bigness of a pocket book', and if the Fifth Monarchy Men had had their way there would have been an entirely new code based on the law of Moses.

Under the Norman and Angevin Kings the Chancery was the secretariat of state. The Chancellor, as Keeper of the Great Seal, by which the royal commands were authenticated, became the legal centre of the constitution; thus it was his responsibility to deal with cases which could not be dealt with by the ordinary courts because the law itself was at fault. By the seventeenth century this equitable jurisdiction of the Chancellors was so widely used that in the reign of James I it seemed to threaten the supremacy of the Common Law courts of King's Bench and Common Pleas. Chancery became associated with the royal prerogative and divine right and so when the Roundheads got the upper hand its very existence was challenged.

During the Commonwealth the seal was in the hands of commissioners and in 1654 Cromwell issued ordinances for the re-organisation of the Court. But two years later these ordinances were allowed to lapse, and when James and John Baker filed their bills in Chancery the Court was in a turmoil of uncertainty and disarray.[1]

They addressed themselves to Chancery because the Common Law courts could only give a remedy when a wrong had already been done.[2] As neither of them claimed the estate until after the deaths of the life tenants, Widow Baker and Henry Oxenden, neither of them had yet suffered any wrong; and as neither was in actual possession, neither could use the normal Common Law procedure of an action for ejectment against the other.

Chancery was therefore the sole available source of remedy, and for the Bakers' purposes it had one great advantage – the evidence of witnesses was taken by written deposition, whereas in the Common Law courts it was taken orally. Both James and John Baker claimed to be the right heir to the estate as great nephews of Robert Baker, but the pedigrees by which they traced their ancestry back to their illustrious forebear were completely different from each other. The issue to be decided was therefore very simple – which pedigree was the true one? The evidence to determine this point consisted, very largely, of the recollections of witnesses who could remember Robert Baker, his family and their doings, either in Somerset or in London. As Robert had been dead for over thirty years, many of these witnesses were extremely old, so it was essential for both James and John to obtain valid written records of the testimony of their witnesses.

But if the written evidence procedure of Chancery could supply a remedy for this difficulty, there was a tremendous counter-balancing disadvantage. The issue to be decided – which claimant was the true great-nephew? – was one of fact, which by Common Law was triable by a jury. In such cases the Lord Chancellor, after hearing the written evidence read to him in court, would formulate the issue to be determined and refer it to the Common Law courts for trial by jury. After the trial the case would be returned to Chancery for a final decree. The expenses of such a suit were therefore likely to be enormous, particularly when many of the witnesses lived a long way from London. First of all, written evidence would have to be taken, and then the witnesses would have to come up to Westminster Hall to give the same evidence orally at the Common Law court. And there was always the possibility of a retrial and that they might have to come more than once, for, as Lord Chancellor Nottingham himself confessed, 'it is grown the reproach of the Chancery that a cause is not half done when it is decreed'.[3]

The suit was started by John Baker, the Wellington shoemaker, whose position as the recognised heir appears to have been challenged by James Baker in the mid 1650s. He filed his bill of complaint stating his claim, and in June 1657 the court, sitting in Westminster Hall, granted him a commission to take the written evidence of his witnesses, many of whom lived 'above 6 score miles distant from this Citty and are aged about foure score yeares, [and] for want of whose testimonys if they should dy the plaintiff will loose his Cause'.[4]

By this time John Baker, or rather his wife, who 'used to mannage his Concernes' for him,[5] had secured the backing of two local gentlemen. The Wescombes and the Seamans lived in the neighbourhood of Milverton and Halse, a few miles west of Taunton and north of Wellington. Aldred Seaman came from Milverton, where he was later to be buried, and was aged about fifty; his family bore their own coat of arms.[6] One of the Wescombes had been a merchant in the City of London and several of them had been admitted to the Middle Temple.[7] John Wescombe was also about fifty years old and described himself as of Tale, in the parish of Payhembury, Devonshire, some twelve miles south of Wellington.[8] He also had a house and probably some land at Hillfarance, half way between Wellington and Taunton, where he and John Baker may have first met.[9]

Seaman and Wescombe did not support John Baker for philanthropic reasons. They hoped to acquire a share of his inheritance when his rights had been successfully established, and both of them did in fact subsequently enjoy for a while an interest in part of the Baker lands in payment for their expenses in the prosecution of John Baker's claim.[10]

John Baker's suit got off to a bad start, for it was found that his bill of complaint had been 'in some particulars mistaken, so as he cannot safely proceede therein to a hearing'.[11] In June 1658 he filed another bill,[12] and William Lenthall, the ex-Speaker of the House of Commons, who was then Master of the Rolls, granted him another commission to examine witnesses.[13] But then the death of the Lord Protector, Oliver Cromwell, on 3 September had caused a tumult of uncertainty in the legal world and the unexecuted commission had had to be renewed in December.[14]

Meanwhile James Baker had been proceeding with his customary efficiency. He was a yeoman, not a penniless journeyman shoemaker like John Baker, and so he did not need any financial help – at first. He lived at Stoney Stratton, just outside Evercreech on the edge of the Mendip Hills between Shepton Mallet and Bruton. Here he owned land looking out westward towards the Vale of Taunton; it was worth eighty pounds a year, and he also had 'a considerable stocke of Cattell',[15] whose descendants motorists may still encounter, wending their leisurely way along the deep narrow lanes between the cider-apple orchards. By May 1658 he had filed his bill of complaint and been granted a commission to examine witnesses.[16]

James Baker's case was extremely simple. Like his rival John Baker he claimed to be Robert Baker's great nephew. But he asserted that Robert, far from being the son of William Baker of Staplegrove and Taunton, had been the youngest son of James's great-grandfather, one John Baker of Chiddesleigh in the parish of Old Cleeve, between Minehead and Williton. This John Baker had had a son, Thomas, whose son John was the father of James Baker of Evercreech, the complainant.[12] If this could all be proved there was no doubt that James was the true heir.

The execution of the commission to take evidence was held on 18 October 1658 at Bruton, probably in a hired room at an inn. The four commissioners, two nominated by James and two by John Baker, were William Smyth, who was active as a Justice of the Peace in Somerset during the Commonwealth, Edward Clarke, who was to become a Justice a few years later, Christopher Overton and Thomas Dyke.[17] The questions or interrogatories to be put to the witnesses had been settled in London by mutual consent of the two Bakers' lawyers, and the commissioners had to adhere to them. They were 'not to take upon them to judge what interrogatories are pertinent and what not, but must examine upon them as they find them'; they were to be completely impartial, and were not 'to leave the room where the witness is examined and go into another room to entertain secret conferences with either of the parties, their attorneys or solicitors'.[18]

The first two witnesses were two young yeomen from Old Cleeve, both in their early thirties. One of them, John Crockford, was the churchwarden there, and the other, Laurence Baker, who had known the complainant James Baker for over twenty years but was apparently not related to him, had previously served in the same office at Old Cleeve. They both deposed that together they had searched the parish register of christenings, marriages and burials and that they had found that one Robert Baker, son of John Baker, had been baptised on 11 November 1562. They had been able to find no other Robert Baker in the register.

The other seven witnesses were all old, several being over eighty. Six of their depositions were very much alike. The most articulate of them, Henry Howe of Stogursey, yeoman, said that he had known the complainant James Baker's father John very well, and had also known his grandfather Thomas for twenty years. The great grandfather's name was John, or so he, Henry Howe 'hath heard by the relation of his Grandfather, grandmother and mother and hath also heard old Mr. Trevillian of Nettlecombe saye the like'.[17]

'Old Mr. Trevillian' was a member of an ancient Cornish family which had acquired a large estate in Nettlecombe through a fortunate marriage in the fifteenth century. Many of them had acted as Justices of the Peace and one had been High Sheriff in the time of James I. Despite the great difference in social status they had evidently been on friendly terms with the yeomen Bakers in the vicinity, one of whom had in 1591 bequeathed to his god-daughter, Elizabeth Trevelyan, 'one ewe hogge'.[19] The Trevelyans were still living in their delectable home at Nettlecombe Court when James Baker's commission was executed at Bruton, and it is perhaps significant that none of them gave evidence on his behalf, although they must have had knowledge of the subject under investigation.

Nettlecombe Court is only one mile from Chidgley, or Chiddesleigh, as it was spelled in the seventeenth century. According to Henry Howe and several other ancient witnesses, Chidgley was 'the place of the family and birth of the Ancestors of all the Bakers'. Here Robert Baker was said to have been born,[17] probably in the long low farmhouse which still stands at the head of a combe in the Brendon Hills, and whose transomed windows and projecting porch look out towards the Quantocks and the distant sea.

The Bakers of Old Cleeve were a very prolific family, and not all of them could live at Chidgley. Robert Baker's eldest brother, Thomas, had (still according to Henry Howe) moved over the hill and settled about a mile away in the next combe, at Leighland Chapel, where even today there is only one farm house. Younger brothers had to make their own way in the world, so Robert and another brother had been brought up as tailors in Old Cleeve; but according to Jesper Hethercott and several other witnesses they both 'went for many years sithence out of their Father's Cuntry when younge men to the Citty of London', and there Robert 'had gotten a good Estate' and lived in the parish of St Martin in the Fields.[17]

The last witness was Joane Younge, a widow of seventy-five who lived in Bruton and claimed to be Robert Baker's first cousin once removed. She had been born in Old Cleeve but had gone when a young woman to live in London. There she had known Robert and 'did often times frequent the house of the said Robert Baker where he then lived in the Strand, who used there the trade of a Taylor'. Joane Younge's brother, Richard Baker, had lived with Robert 'and was foreman of his shopp', and this was why she had often visited her cousin's house, where she had heard him say 'that he was borne in Old Cleeve'.[17]

The testimony of these nine witnesses, taken at Bruton on 18 October 1658, was all the evidence that James Baker was able to collect in Somerset to support his claim to be the great nephew of Robert Baker of Old Cleeve, a tailor who had gone to London early in life. Much of it was based on half-forgotten hearsay, and each witness was careful to qualify his remarks with such phrases as 'he hath heard', or 'he hath heard it said', or 'by report'. With the exception of Joane Younge they had virtually no knowledge of what had become of Robert Baker in London; they did not mention Piccadilly either as an article of dress or as the name of Robert's house, and even Henry Howe could only say that 'hee lived in or neare London, but in what place the said Robert dwelled this deponent [i.e., witness] doth not now well remember'. In fact this Robert Baker seems to have been thoroughly stand-offish towards his country relations, for when one of his elder brothers called on him in London Robert is said to have 'bidd him goe home about his business and trouble him noe more'.[17]

There is another difficulty too – why was the commission held at Bruton? No doubt Bruton was convenient for Joane Younge, who lived there, and for James Baker himself, who lived nearby at Evercreech. But all the other eight witnesses lived thirty or forty miles away, at Old Cleeve or Stogursey or Bishop's Lydeard, and six of them were old. James Baker must have had to pay for their travelling expenses, so why did he arrange for his evidence to be taken so far away from his family's home at Old Cleeve? Could it be that he was afraid that if the commission was held there, unwanted witnesses might appear, and demand to be heard?

Unfortunately it is now possible to check the accuracy of only one item in the whole of the Bruton evidence. Apart from the family tree put forward on James Baker's behalf and the assertion that Robert was baptised at Old Cleeve on 11 November 1562 there are no hard facts capable of being checked from any available source. And even the family tree cannot be verified, for the parish registers of Old Cleeve no longer exist for the years prior to 1660, and the records of the Bakers' wills (if they made any) were destroyed by bombing at Exeter during the last war. But there is just one statement that can be checked – the statement of John Crockford, churchwarden of Old Cleeve, that he had searched the parish register with Laurence Baker, and apart from the baptismal entry of 11 November 1562, could find no other entry relating to Robert Baker. Every parish was compelled by law to send a copy of the entries in its register to the bishop; some of these transcripts still survive in fragmentary form and are now in the Somerset Record Office at Taunton. The transcripts for Old Cleeve show that one Robert Baker was churchwarden there in 1606, and that he was buried on 1 June 1636. Crockford's statement was therefore untrue; and moreover it seems almost certain that he must have known it was untrue.

5 *A Long Day at the Fountain in Taunton*

Three months after James Baker's evidence had been taken at Bruton the same four commissioners assembled on 10 January 1659 at the Fountain tavern, near the castle in Taunton, to execute John Baker's commission.[1] This was a much more elaborate affair than the Bruton session, and the evidence gushed out like cider from a broken cask. There were about 150 questions to be addressed to each of the twelve witnesses, eleven of whom appeared for John Baker. It was upon the evidence taken on this day that John Baker's case chiefly depended.

Eight of his witnesses had been related to Robert Baker, either by blood or by marriage, and six of them had known him personally. Most of their evidence was therefore based on first-hand knowledge, not hearsay. Some of them could not recollect the full family pedigree, but all of them testified to at least part of the account already given on earlier pages – that Robert Baker was a younger son of William Baker of Staplegrove, that after his father's death he had lived in Taunton with his elder brother, also William, and that he had gone to London, where he had become 'a verie rich man'; John Baker, who now claimed the estate, was William's grandson.

In support of these bare facts they produced a considerable body of circumstantial evidence about Robert Baker's doings, mostly in Somerset, some of which has already been mentioned. Thomas Stamperow of Taunton St Mary, 'cordwinder, aged fowerscore yeares or thereabouts', for instance, said that Robert's elder brother, William, had been a mercer or linen draper in Taunton and had lived in 'a certaine house between the red Lyon and the Beare'. Robert had lived with and worked with his brother and when Stamperow had first met him he was about sixteen years old. The witness had known Robert for about three or four years before the latter's departure to London, and could remember all this because Robert's brother had married a relative of his, Joane Gibbons.

Peter Slade, a tailor of Bradford-on-Tone near Taunton, aged about eighty, said that he had often gone with Robert and William Baker to the markets of nearby towns to help sell William's wares; and 'when the sickness or plague happened into the Towne of Taunton about threescore and eight years sithence', William and Robert had come to live with the witness's mother in a rented house at Shattern, then on the outskirts of the town. This outbreak of plague took place in 1592-3, and caused over 230 deaths in the parish of St Mary Magdalene alone.

The next witness was Mary Wallen, wife of a Taunton worsted comber. She was aged sixty-four, and was a niece of Robert Baker, his brother William being her father. The latter had died while she was still an infant and so 'she had not the happiness to know him'. But her mother had told her that her uncle Robert was the son of William Baker of Staplegrove, that he had been 'brought up and educated under and by his brother' William the mercer, and later been apprenticed to a tailor in London.

Emanuel Mico, a clothier of Taunton St James, aged sixty, had been 'cousin German' to Robert Baker. He had served as one of the parish overseers of the poor and was able to read. He believed that Robert was the son of one William Baker because he had 'seene a Transcript of an ancient writing testifying the same'. He was not able to produce this vital document, which has not come to light even now. But in support of his conviction about Robert's paternity he also mentioned an entry in the court rolls of the Manor of Taunton Priory and Canon Street, whereby William Baker immediately prior to his death had surrendered a house in Taunton to Robert; he certified that a transcript of this entry was a true copy, and the enrollment of this document is now in the Somerset Record Office.[2]

The evidence taken at the Fountain was not, however, confined to the Baker pedigree and Robert's early life at Taunton. Unlike the witnesses for James Baker at Bruton, who knew practically nothing of Robert's later career apart from his wealth, several of John Baker's witnesses were very well informed about later events. Old Thomas Stamperow, who had never been to London himself, had often heard that Robert had lived near Charing Cross 'neere London' and that he 'had gotten a great estate by makeinge of Pickadilly Collers'. But Peter Slade had been to London at least once, and there he had seen and spoken to Robert. Moreover his sister had often given him news of Robert, for she had married one of the yeomen of the guard and lived in London for fifty years; so he was able to say that Robert had been bound apprentice to a tailor in the Strand and had lived between York House and the New Exchange (i.e. Britain's Burse).

Mary Wallen said that although he had been a tailor Robert had also been 'owner of divers Bricke Kilnes, and by his Trade and Industrie gott a great estate'. Her brother John, who had been a shoemaker in Wellington and was one of Robert's nephews, had lived with his uncle at Piccadilly Hall for a time, and a relative of hers who had been an attorney at law and 'frequented the termes att London did often bringe tydings and consideracions' to Mary's mother. This evidence of nephew John's visit to his uncle was confirmed by John's widow, Elizabeth Baker, aged sixty, who lived at Staplegrove with her daughter. She recalled that her husband, one of the shoemakers of Wellington, did twice 'repaire thence to London' to see his uncle, with whom he had been 'verie intimatelie acquainted', and who had entertained him 'very loveinglie'. On one of these visits Robert Baker had given his nephew a bond for a debt of three pounds which a relative in Bridgwater owed him, together with a letter of attorney empowering John Baker to take payment of the debt. The originals of both these documents were produced at the Fountain for Elizabeth Baker to identify, which she did.

Emanuel Mico, whose business as a clothier probably took him to London, had been to Robert's house in the Strand and 'diverse times did meete and drinke with the said

Robert Baker in the Cities of London and Westminster'. Yet another John Baker, this one being a mariner from Bridgwater, aged sixty-three and a first cousin of Robert's, testified to the convivial hospitality at Piccadilly Hall. When he had called there about forty years ago (i.e., in about 1618) Robert was not at home, but as he was returning to his lodgings near Temple Bar John Baker had met his cousin in the fields near Picca-dilly. Robert had immediately 'owned him to be his Kinsman', invited him back to Piccadilly Hall and entertained him very courteously. His host had enquired for news of John's mother and of 'all the rest of his several friends in Bridgwater and Taunton', but had not mentioned any kinsmen at Old Cleeve. This was merely one of several visits to Robert, who always gave his cousin 'beere and sacke', for he was 'a verie Riche man'.

Perhaps the most convincing of all the evidence given during that winter day at the Fountain referred to the visits which Robert Baker had made to Taunton after he had gone to live in London. There were three such visits, and at any rate by the time of the second and third he had become rich and famous, and his return to his native town caused a stir which his friends and relations naturally remembered very clearly. Ro-bert's first visit evidently took place in 1599 and his main purpose was, as three witnesses testified, to sell the cottage in Taunton which he had inherited from his father. His niece Mary Wallen said that the house was in Middle Street and was sold to one King-esbury, while Emanuel Mico the clothier did not say where the house was in Taunton but only that it had been sold to one French. The deed of surrender of a house in Canon Street to John French was entered on the manorial court rolls, where Robert's signature, or rather his initials, may still be seen in the Somerset Record Office.[3]

But Robert's visits also had a philanthropic purpose. His elder brother, William the mercer, had married in 1591 [4] and his wife Joane had borne him two sons and two daughters. William had, however, died before 1600 while still in his twenties, and although his widow had subsequently been married again, to one Thomas Manning, Robert Baker as the prosperous uncle evidently felt that he had some responsibility for the four young children. Roger Manning, a child of Joane's second marriage, remem-bered that Robert Baker had visited his father's house in Taunton and that Roger's two half-brothers did 'call the said Robert Baker uncle'; and Robert had tipped young Roger with 'a peece of gold'.

One of the later visits to Taunton was occasioned by the death of the four children's mother, Joane. They were thus left dependent on their stepfather, Thomas Manning, and so Uncle Robert 'came from London unto Taunton and lodged at the Three Cupps', possibly in about 1610. The Three Cups was later known as the London Inn and is now the County Hotel. There was quite a family gathering to discuss the children's future, for two of Robert's sisters were also there – Elizabeth, and Susan, who had married Mr William Blake, uncle of the future Admiral Robert Blake, and lived in Bridgwater. Emanuel Mico senior, who was parish clerk at Taunton St James's and a relative of the family by marriage, was also at the Three Cups, and Robert had sent him to fetch one of the children, Mary, who had been apprenticed in the town. When she arrived Robert had 'Kissed and imbraced her and acknowledged her to be his Kinsman', and given her some money. Aunt Elizabeth or Aunt Susan had said 'that it was pitty that such a Girle . . . should milke the Cow and serve the house', as apprentices often had to do, and Uncle Robert had then asked Mary 'whether she would goe alonge with him to London to live with him there, who answered she could not, in regard she was an apprentice then in Taunton St. James'.

The two boys, William and John, who later became shoemakers in Wellington, were also summoned to the Three Cups. So too was their half-brother, Roger Manning, who remembered that Robert Baker did 'admonishe and advise and did make much of' his two nephews, and tell them that as 'their father was dead they should have care of their business and be good boyes'. Whether he gave them any money on this occasion is not recorded, but he probably did so, for Emanuel Mico junior, who was only a relative by marriage, remembered that Robert had given him 'and his brother and his three sisters six pence a peece' and asked young Emanuel 'if he would goe to London with him, saying that if he would he would keepe him in his family . . . and make a Taylor of him'.

Robert Baker's favourite was evidently his niece Mary. She recalled how her uncle had taken her, as a girl of about sixteen, 'alonge with him to walke, expressing that he was very desirous to see the old places called Poles Bridge and the French weare that he was formerly acquainted with, . . . and used to walke unto when he formerly lived with his brother William Baker, a Mercer'. Pole's, or Paul's, Bridge was in the parish of Bishop's Hull just outside Taunton; at French Weir, which still exists, the River Tone divides into two streams to flow through the town and join together lower down. To-day one can still slip out of the noisy streets of Taunton to walk along the path beside the Tone to French Weir, and listen to the steady placid sound of falling water which Robert Baker and his niece heard there three hundred and fifty years ago.

After his return to London Robert did not forget his niece. On several occasions he sent her 'divers Tokens (to witt), one peece of Gold of Twentie or Two and Twentie shillings', which was brought to her by Mr William Chaplin's wife. Mr Chaplin probably went to London on business from time to time, as also did Mr Mayne, who lived at Trull, near Taunton, and who on another occasion brought Mary twenty shillings in silver from her uncle. Later, when she had married Noah Wallen, a worsted comber, Robert sent her a letter desiring her husband to take possession of a piece of ground near Holway Lane in Taunton, and promising that he would build a house for her there.

Robert must have enjoyed his visits to his native haunts. He had become a local celebrity, and his niece Mary remembered with awe how Mr Andrew Hendley, 'one of the first and sufficientist men in the Towne', and later to become Taunton's first Mayor, had invited her uncle to dine with him. Mr Thomas Brereton, too, a Justice of the Peace and in 1620 and 1622 one of Taunton's two Members of Parliament, had invited Baker 'to supp with him'. This event made a great impression on Mrs Brereton, for she afterwards told Mary that 'she would never forgett it by reason of a jest that the said Robert Baker then put forth att Supper; he then carving of a Breast of Mutton said to the said Mrs. Bruton [sic], will you have the Tip next the horne'. It is not clear whether Mrs Brereton remembered the remark because she was amused or because she was shocked.

All the evidence given at the Fountain which has so far been mentioned was based on recollections of events that had taken place very many years earlier. But two of the witnesses also provided first-hand information about events which had occurred after Robert's death. The first of these witnesses was again his niece Mary Wallen, who had lived in London for a year and while there had been to see 'her Aunt Baker' (Robert's widow, Mary) at Piccadilly Hall. The Widow Baker had treated her kindly, acknowledged her as Robert's niece, and even said that she 'did resemble the said Robert Baker . . . in countenance'. The purpose of young Mary's visit was clearly to find out whether her uncle had left her anything in his will. When she eventually asked the all-important question Widow Baker had replied that 'for ought she knew the said Robert Baker . . . had not given her any thinge att his death', but added that the children of Mary's brother William, one of the Wellington shoemakers, might be 'the better for his estate in case they live'. Perhaps in order to get rid of her Widow Baker had eventually given her ten shillings 'and bid her see the City and come to her againe, which she accordinglie did'.

The other witness was Amye, or Anne, Gardiner, aged thirty-six, who was the wife of John Gardiner, the minister at Staplegrove. Amye was a great-niece of Robert Baker, being the daughter of John Baker, one of the Wellington shoemakers. About eight years previously, or around 1650, she too had been in London and had 'had speech' with Widow Baker at Piccadilly Hall. The widow had acknowledged her as a kinswoman of Robert's and well remembered Amye's late father, John the shoemaker. He had lived with his uncle Robert at Piccadilly Hall when a young man, and the Widow Baker had evidently had a soft spot for him – 'she did very well love' John Baker, 'for that he loved her child verie well during the time he lived with her husband'. One gets the impression, however, that this interview between Widow Baker and Amye Gardiner was not very cordial. The widow had had a lot of trouble with Inigo Jones and the Privy Council about the water at Piccadilly, Edward Hubert had already claimed part of the estate, and here was this Mrs Gardiner come obviously to see how the land lay. From long experience Widow Baker knew how to deal with situations like this, and even how to turn them to her own advantage; for she suggested to her young visitor that if Amye's cousin John (Robert's great-nephew, on whose behalf all the evidence at the Fountain was being taken) would commit his reversionary interest in the whole estate to her, Widow Baker, then 'she would use him the said John Baker . . . verie well'.

Amye Gardiner was a silly woman and probably did not notice the cloven hoof revealed by this proposal. As a great-niece of Robert Baker she was naturally a supporter of her cousin John Baker's claim to the inheritance of the estate, but as well as giving evidence herself she also sought out other possible witnesses and even suggested to them what they should testify. This appears at least to be the implication of a long series of questions which the lawyers of the rival claimant, James Baker of Evercreech, had intended should be put to her and other witnesses for John Baker at the Fountain. For some unexplained reason none of these questions were answered by any of the witnesses, but their mere existence introduces the first unmistakable suggestion of chicanery in the lawsuit of James versus John Baker.

The purpose of James Baker's questions was to elicit evidence that he, James Baker, had recently visited the parish clerk at Staplegrove to see whether the register contained any entries about Robert Baker of Taunton, whose existence, or at any rate whose connexion with Robert Baker of Piccadilly Hall, he completely denied. The parish clerk's wife, so the questions imply, had told James Baker that her husband had the register, but when her husband appeared he was very angry with his wife and denied that he had the book. This had been done on the orders of the minister of Staplegrove, John Gardiner, or rather of his indiscreet wife Amye, cousin of James Baker's opponent John Baker.

In the light of later events it is ironical that the first accusation of conspiracy to defeat the course of justice should have been made by James Baker, but his affairs were always better managed than John's. A very sinister interpretation can, indeed, be placed on this episode of the Staplegrove register, which will be referred to later. But there is also a very simple explanation of it which may be correct. There was in fact no entry about Robert Baker in the register; Amye Gardiner knew of this unfortunate gap in her cousin John Baker's case and so tried to conceal it from the prying eyes of his rival James.

The object of this unseemly quarrel, the register, still exists, until recently in the safe and kindly keeping of the Rector of Staplegrove, and now in that of the Somerset Record Office. It is a long thin volume, its parchment leaves crinkled and yellow with age. The first entry dates from 1558. There are three references to the Bakers – the christenings of James in 1568, of Anthony in 1570 and of William in 1571, all sons of William Baker. There is nothing more – no Robert Baker.

There was, however, one piece of unquestionably reliable documentary evidence which John Baker could and did produce – namely the entry in the Taunton manorial court rolls of 1584 which showed (as stated earlier) that a William Baker had existed, and that shortly before his death he had surendered his house in Canon Street to his youngest son Robert.[2] This was certainly useful evidence for John Baker's case, but oddly enough some more came from a witness called on behalf of James Baker. He was Anthony Mapowder of Shepton Mallett, gentleman, aged thirty-eight, who briefly testified that he had searched the registers of both Taunton St Mary and Taunton St James, and had found that four Robert Bakers had been baptised there but only three buried. The object of this evidence was to confuse the issue and imply that John Baker's witnesses had not all been talking about the same person. But looked at from another point of view it provides negative evidence for John's case, for it proved beyond doubt that one Robert Baker, born in Taunton, had gone away and died elsewhere.

6 The Case Comes On

Anthony Mapowder was the last witness to depose at the Fountain, and by the time he had finished the candles must have burnt very low on that winter day. The great strength of John Baker's evidence was that so many of his witnesses had themselves known Robert Baker. For them Robert Baker of Taunton had been a real person whose early life and later celebrity they had watched with lively interest, totally different from the vague shadowy figure of James Baker's Robert of Old Cleeve. But there was also a great weakness in John's case – the absence of any certain record of Robert's baptism in the parish registers, for they could not say which of the four Roberts christened in Taunton was to be identified with the builder of Piccadilly Hall.

After all this evidence had been collected in Somerset the testimony of other witnesses was taken in London for information about Robert Baker's career there. This London evidence was taken in February and April 1659 at the office of the Chancery examiner.[1] Most of it was given on behalf of James Baker, and one item in it can be proved to be wrong. Paul Bettering, aged seventy-two, and John Harris, aged sixty, both describing themselves as gentlemen, were evidently shown transcripts from the registers of St Martin in the Fields which purported to relate to Robert Baker's two marriages there. Both Bettering and Harris said that Baker's first wife was a flaxwoman named Katherine, and Bettering said that he had himself been present at this wedding, 'beinge of [Baker's] Acquaintance'. Now the only marriage recorded in the registers between a Robert Baker and a woman named Katherine occurs in 1585, before Bettering was even born.[2] The woman's maiden name was Evans, and it is certain that this Robert Baker was not the same person as the later Robert Baker of Piccadilly Hall. We have already seen that the latter had a daughter called Judith by his first wife; and when Judith died many years later she bequeathed an annuity of ten pounds to her uncle, John Nightingale.[3] So her mother's maiden name had been Nightingale, not Evans. The registers of St Martin in the Fields show that Robert Baker married Elizabeth (not Katherine) Nightingale on 16 November 1600.[4]

James Baker or his lawyers had evidently searched the registers of St Martin in the Fields, found that a Robert Baker had married there in 1585, and assumed, without searching any further, that this entry referred to the right Robert. This date of marriage, 1585, fitted chronologically very well with the evidence already given on James Baker's behalf to the commission at Bruton that Robert Baker had been baptised at Old Cleeve in 1562. Better still, it appeared to invalidate the evidence given on John

43

Baker's behalf at Taunton that Robert Baker was a younger brother of William Baker, who had been baptised at Staplegrove in 1571.

James Baker's Robert was in fact supposed to have been born twenty years before John's Robert. This supposition also fitted very well with the statement made by three of James's witnesses that Robert had served at Tilbury camp during the Armada crisis of 1588. One of them, Elizabeth Robinson, said that he had served at Tilbury with her father, and added that both of them were newly married at the time.[1]

In face of these discrepancies it is very difficult to know what credibility can be attached to the rest of James Baker's London witnesses. This is a pity, because their evidence is the principal source for much of Robert's London career. A great deal of it was only hearsay, but it is possible that they had mixed their recollection of the early career of the Robert Baker who married Katherine Evans in 1585 with that of Robert later of Piccadilly Hall. It seems unlikely that they simply made it all up; several points in it have indeed been satisfactorily checked, and much of it does fit in with what is known from other sources.

Part of their evidence has already been mentioned in Chapter 1. There were nine witnesses, all of whom except a young lawyer (called to certify a copy of Robert's will) were aged between fifty-six and seventy-two. The general tenor of their statements was that Robert had come to London from Somerset when still a young man, that he was already a tailor by trade when he arrived, and that at first (according to Paul Bettering) he had worked as a journeyman for Mr Brales at the Flying Horse in the Strand, where he clubbed with other journeymen of Somerset extraction. Then, after perhaps serving under the Earl of Essex in the expedition to Cadiz in 1596, he had married a poor flaxwoman and moved to St Martin's Lane, where Elizabeth Andrews, then a girl of ten living 'within foare dores or thereabouts' of his house, remembered him as a poor tailor. After a while he had moved back to the Strand, to the sign of the Seven Stars, 'his said then wiffe Keepinge a flaxe Shoppe there'. Here, with the help of his wife, 'a verie Carefull good woman', he had started making 'Pickadillys', had 'gott good stoar of money' thereby, and 'kept many men att worke'. Subsequently he had 'purchased Lands of Kinge James lying neere the Tennis Courte, and which was afterwards by Queene Anne [of Denmark] . . . named or called Pickadilly'. After the death of his first wife he had married Mary, daughter of Mr Higgins, an apothecary who lived near the Savoy.

The most interesting evidence was that of Jane Jeames, aged sixty-six, the wife of a plasterer. She had lived and worked at Piccadilly Hall for three or four years as a servant while Robert Baker was still alive and living there 'as a gentleman upon his meanes'. She remembered his saying that 'hee was a Somersetshire man and was apprenticed there to a Taylor and learned the trade before ever hee came to London'. And 'in his Fashinge and Merriment with his said wiffe Mary hee would sometimes speake to her to ye effecte following, to witt, Moll, pray lett us have a white pott made of Milk and as we have it in our Countrie, for you knowe I am a Somersettshire man, and where else should hee bin [i.e. I have been] borne', or words to the same effect.[1]

The most important thing about this London evidence given for James Baker was that all of it except those parts relating to Robert Baker's first marriage, which are untrue, and to his military service at Tilbury, which are very doubtful, can also be used to support the case for John Baker. James's London witnesses knew that Robert had come from Somerset, but none of them said that he came from Old Cleeve; and the evidence of Jane Jeames quoted above even implies that he came from Taunton, for the words which she attributed to Robert contain a distinct echo of a saying peculiar to the inhabitants of the fertile area round about known as Taunton Dean. There the natives were so proud of their origin that they had 'a boastful proverb, "Where should I be born else but in Taunton Dean?" as if it were a disparagement to be born in any other place; and none in England, nay in the whole world, were to be compared with it'.[5]

The great weakness of John Baker's evidence taken at the Fountain in Taunton was, as we have seen, that he could produce no certain record of Robert's baptism. John's lawyers had, however, got hold of a bond and a letter of attorney signed by Robert and given to one of his nephews, and the validity of this document had been attested by a relative at the Fountain. In February 1659 the lawyers produced these documents at the office of the Chancery examiner, together with further evidence in support of their authenticity. John Cooper, aged seventy-nine, a barber who 'did use sometimes to trimme' Robert Baker, said that he had known John Dodd, a public scrivener, now dead. He testified that the two papers were in Dodd's handwriting, and that Dodd had been 'verie honest in ye transaction business'. Francis Bury, aged seventy-four, a scrivener who had been apprenticed to Dodd, stated that he had known Robert and his hand. Robert used to come to Dodd's house in the Strand and employ him as a scrivener in business matters. He testified his belief that the signatures on the two deeds were in Robert Baker's own true hand.[6]

The other witnesses produced in London on John's behalf gave evidence about the numerous deaths in the Baker family after Robert's death. In view of the absolute refusal of his second wife, Mary, the Widow Baker, who was still living at Piccadilly Hall, to give evidence for either James or John Baker — a refusal which she somehow maintained to the very end of her life – it is significant that her brother and her rent collector both testified for John. Arnold Higgins the brother's only interesting remark was that his brother-in-law Robert had been about forty-five years old when he died, which would place his birth about 1578, some sixteen years later than the date which had been asserted on James Baker's behalf. William Prescott, the rent collector for Widow Baker's part of the estate, said that his wife had been related to Robert's first wife, but could give no details about her.[6]

By the summer of 1659 all the evidence had been taken, the depositions had been submitted to the Court of Chancery, and both James and John Baker were ready at last for the case to go forward. Monday, 13 June 1659, was appointed as the day for the hearing, which was held in Westminster Hall. 'Upon which Day the said Causes comeinge to be heard before the Right Honourable the Lords Commissioners for the

Great Seale of England in the presence of Councell learned on all sides', both James and John appeared and claimed to be the rightful heir to the estate. This was a question of fact, triable in a Common Law court by a jury, so the Lords Commissioners directed that a trial should be had in the Court of King's Bench in the next Michaelmas term, and that afterwards the two parties should resort back to Chancery for a further order.[7]

Elaborate preparations for the trial had to be made. In a Common Law court witnesses had to give their evidence orally, and submit to cross-examination. So the twenty people who had testified at Bruton or Taunton, most of them old and some of them very old, had to be fetched up to London, housed, and brought to Westminster Hall at the appointed day and hour. There were also another thirteen witnesses living nearby in the western suburbs. There were counsel and attorneys innumerable, plus their West Country agents such as Anthony Mapowder who had searched the Taunton parish registers and later delivered the writs of *sub poena* to James Baker's Somerset witnesses. John Baker's patrons were there too – John Wescombe and Aldred Seaman, plus at least one well-wisher, Gustavus Venner, a young gentleman from Wellington.[8] On the day before the trial James Baker tried to *sub poena* the Widow Baker herself. One of his agents was sent to Piccadilly Hall with a writ, but 'being not admytted to speake' with her, he tried to tip one of the servants to accept notification of the summons. Widow Baker had evidently foreseen this contingency and given instructions that nothing was to be accepted; so the messenger had to leave the writ and the proffered shilling on the doorstep and go away; and 'the said Mary Baker appeared not at the said Tryall'.[9]

The trial took place on 8 and 9 November 1659. All the witnesses who were present were examined. John Wescombe stated later that 'the tryall was very longe and either party [was] heard untill theyre respective Councell did declare they had noe more to say'. At last the jury retired, but by the time they had reached their verdict it was so late that the judge had adjourned the court and gone home. They therefore delivered a 'privy verdict', which meant that they gave their decision to the judge privately out of court. On the next morning, when the court re-assembled to hear the jury publicly proclaim their verdict, James Baker and his counsel had evidently got wind from one of the jurymen of what the verdict was or else decided that they had no hope of success; so they did not appear when summoned, although one of James's barristers, Mr Serjeant Twydon, was present in court to hear what happened. This legal subterfuge, known as suffering a non-suit, meant that the plaintiff (James) renounced the suit but after paying the defendant's costs he could begin the action again. The purpose of a non-suit was to deprive the opposing party of a favourable verdict.[10]

So John Baker had been tricked, although quite legitimately by the standards of justice then prevailing. James of course had no intention of conceding the contest and on the very next day after the trial, when the witnesses were beginning their journey home, possibly rather bewildered, appliction was made to Chancery for the case to be referred back to that court. The result of the trial was reported to Chancery in February

1660 – the clerk who entered the record made a mistake and wrote 'A verdict passed for the said John Baker' and then crossed this out and substituted 'James Baker was non suite' – and in the following July James Baker's counsel asked for a second trial.[11]

By this time the Commonwealth had come to an end and Charles II had returned from his exile. Sir Edward Hyde, later Earl of Clarendon, had been appointed Chancellor on 1 June 1660, and he presided over the hearing to decide what should be done next. The grounds for James's application were that three of his witnesses had not appeared at the trial in the preceding November, and that subsequently four more witnesses with material knowledge had been found.[12] John Baker's lawyers replied that as the absent witnesses' depositions had been examined in Chancery, they could have been read in King's Bench, and that James had had plenty of time to discover all possible evidence. They also demanded that their client's costs should be paid before a second trial should be ordered. In the course of the ensuing legal wrangle the Widow Baker, who had been made a nominal party in the James and John suit in order to try to extract evidence from her, was ordered to deposit all the title deeds of the estate in the custody of the court. Whether she ever did so is not known. Ultimately James Baker was ordered to pay his rival's costs and then proceed to another trial at King's Bench. This second trial was to be final for James if it went against him, but if the case went against John he could demand a rehearing.[13]

The second King's Bench trial was held in Westminster Hall on 16 and 17 November 1660. The witnesses – or at any rate most of them – were brought up from Somerset again, and Edward Hubert, son of Robert Baker's daughter Frances, was fetched in a coach from his house in Holborn.[14] John Baker's agents had found a new witness, Thomas Syle, an old shoemaker from Wellington, and he came too, but when they delivered the *sub poena* summoning cousin John Baker (the Bridgwater mariner) they privately gave him twenty shillings and told him to 'goe into Wales', for they feared that he was an unreliable witness and 'would make a fowle house if he came to London to the said tryall'.[15]

The trial began shortly after eight o'clock in the morning. John Baker's evidence was given first, he being the plaintiff in this action, but not all James's witnesses were examined, 'the tyme not giveing leave, it being late, about one a Clock, before ye evidence was ended'. Five hours for the examination of some twenty or thirty witnesses does not seem long by modern standards, but it was certainly thought to be long then. In due course the jury retired, and once more they gave a privy verdict to the judge after the adjournment of the court.[15] On the following morning the court reassembled, the jury answered their names and the secondary, or clerk of the court, asked them whether they adhered to their privy verdict and wished the crier to call the plaintiff, John Baker. This was the usual procedure for the public proclamation of a privy verdict; the plaintiff was summoned first, but this did not mean that the jury had decided in his favour. Unfortunately one of the jurymen did not know this, and when he heard the secondary call for the plaintiff, John, he interrupted and said that their verdict was for the defendant, James. Whereupon Mr Aldred Seaman, John

Baker's solicitor, jumped with great presence of mind to his feet and announced that 'wee do not appeare. And so the plaintiff suffered himselfe to be Non suited'.[16]

Both parties had now been tricked out of a favourable verdict, so once again they resorted back to Chancery for further direction. With his cousin and namesake the Bridgwater mariner now safely out of the way in Wales John Baker claimed that his case had been prejudiced by the absence of this witness, and that four other of his witnesses had been present at the trial but were not examined; two of these, both elderly shoemakers from Wellington, had been 'to his greate Costs brought upp out of the County of Somersett' to testify for him. And more recently he had discovered two more witnesses – Edward Hubert and Alexander Foweraker.[17] He therefore prayed for another trial. James Baker claimed that he too had new witnesses to examine, and demanded payment of his costs. Costs, indeed, seem to have been the main point of interest to the court in deciding what should be done next. Money was running low, so John's request for a new trial was granted, but both parties were to provide security for payment of each other's costs in the event of an unfavourable verdict.[18]

This third trial was held in the Court of Common Pleas in the spring of 1661. 'After a long and full evidence' the jury gave their verdict for John Baker.[19]

7 *The Break-up of the Estate*

After this setback James Baker seems to have decided to give up the contest. Nothing more is heard about him for more than three and a half years, and he would probably never have resumed his suit if he had not been prompted to do so by a powerful backer in London. But despite the advantage which he had gained in the trial in the Court of Common Pleas John Baker had not fully established his title to the estate. His lawyers thought that the best policy was to let sleeping dogs lie, for they made no application to Chancery for further directions or for a final decree, and in 1663 John Baker began to sell his reversionary interest piecemeal in order to pay the debts incurred in the suit so far. In March he sold two of Robert Baker's houses in the Strand for £250, subject of course to the life interests of Widow Baker and Henry Oxenden, and covenanted with the purchaser – optimistically as events turned out – that his interests in the property was 'a good, sure, sole, perfect, absolute, rightfull and indefeasible estate of inheritance in fee simple'.[1] A few weeks later he moved from Wellington in Somerset, where he had lived as a shoemaker, to Payhembury, a remote village some twelve miles south of Wellington in the county of Devon. Here, in the even more remote hamlet of Tale, lived his principal supporter, John Wescombe, one of whose sons is commemorated by a tablet in the church of St Mary. Even today there are only about a dozen houses in Tale, and one is more likely to meet a tractor or a herd of cows than a car in the deeply-sunk narrow lanes.

It must have been very tempting for him to sell his inheritance, although it was clearly disadvantageous for him to do so, for he only had a reversionary interest and his title even to that had not been finally established. His lawyers were clamouring for payment and there was no talk of any further action by James Baker. In his own humble pathetic words he was 'poore and ignorant and wanting freinds',[2] and it is therefore not surprising that this unfortunate and bewildered man succumbed to the temptation. In August 1663 he sold his interest in some of the land near Piccadilly Hall to Edmund Vintner, a doctor of physic, for £180,[3] and a few weeks later he was paid £120 for two houses in the Blue Mews to the south of Leicester Square.[4]

The proceeds of these sales were probably far below the real value of the properties involved. Clearly the most advantageous people for John Baker to sell to were the life tenants, Widow Baker and Henry Oxenden, for by purchasing his reversionary interest they would obtain an estate in fee simple, subject only to such doubts as they might have about John's own title. Widow Baker was not a suitable prospective purchaser, for she had relatively little money, but Henry Oxenden was rich. So John Baker travelled all the way from Devonshire to Oxenden's house at Deane, near Canterbury, to persuade him to buy. Henry's services to the parliamentary cause during the Civil War had been rewarded with a knighthood by Charles II at the Restoration, when he also became one of the Members of Parliament for Sandwich. Eventually he came to London [2] and agreed with John Baker and his lawyers to buy the reversion of three and a half acres of land on the east side of the Haymarket for £2200.[5] This was where Simon Osbaldeston had built his gambling house and bowling greens in the 1630's, and it was through this unfortunate transaction that James Baker's claims were to be revived in far more dangerous form.

By the middle of 1664 John Baker had sold his interest in a large part of the whole estate. William Prescott, formerly Widow Baker's rent collector, who had given evidence for John Baker in 1659, bought a few houses near Piccadilly Hall,[6] and several other small pieces of ground were sold too.[7] John Baker's West Country backers got their cut of course, for John Wescombe bought the reversion of six acres in the vicinity of the modern Golden Square,[8] and he and Aldred Seaman also bought Sir Henry Oxenden's life interest in this ground,[9] thereby obtaining an estate in fee simple, subject, of course, to the validity of John Baker's title.

Only a small part of the proceeds of these sales can ever have reached John Baker, for by the summer of 1663 he had become involved in litigation once again. A new claimant, one George Baker, had appeared,[10] and another commission for the examination of witnesses had been granted by the Court of Chancery. Who George Baker was, or what his claim, is not known, but he proved to be no match even for poor ignorant John Baker.

It was arranged that this new commission should again be executed at the hospitable Fountain tavern in Taunton, on Tuesday 15 September 1663, under the supervision of four commissioners. On the day appointed one of John's commissioners, Robert Cannon, a farmer from Fitzhead, had to execute a commission in another Chancery case, and this being 'like to require his Attendance for a longer tyme than hee expected', John's backers, Wescombe and Seaman, decided to adjourn their commission until the next day. But on the Wednesday Cannon was still unavailable, and George Baker's counsel, who were staying at the Swan in Taunton, became extremely annoyed – they had other business and now refused to join in the commission. Short sharp legal messages passed to and fro between the party waiting at the Fountain and the party fuming at the Swan, and ultimately the commission was executed by Cannon alone, for one of the other commissioners, William Doble, an old Puritan from Timberscombe, had meanwhile fallen sick and died very soon afterwards.[11]

The fact that the only commissioner present was one of those chosen by John Baker, and that all the witnesses who gave evidence were also for John, looked suspicious. At any rate George Baker thought so, and his counsel subsequently alleged at a hearing in Chancery that the commission had been irregularly executed. The matter was referred to one of the clerks of the court for examination, but he reported that nothing improper had been done, and the depositions taken by Cannon at the Fountain were therefore accepted as valid.[12]

There were ten witnesses, five of whom were related to John Baker either by blood or marriage; all of these five relatives had already testified at the first commission at the Fountain five years before. None of the unrelated witnesses had given evidence before; four of them were shoemakers from Wellington, and old. Much of the testimony merely amplified that given in 1658; much of it was concerned with Robert Baker's visits to Taunton and with visits by his relatives to Piccadilly Hall.[13]

Mary Wallen, a niece of Robert Baker, again recalled her uncle's visit to Taunton after the death of her father, William, the mercer. He had summoned his nephews and nieces to the Three Cups and given 'them all some moneyes and charged them to serve God and told them that they should want for nothing'. Then he had gone on to Stogursey to see his other niece, Thomasin, who was a servant there to Mr Hobbs, and had returned to London via Bridgwater, where he visited his cousins. Anne Gent, aged eighty-eight, the wife of a Taunton tailor, confirmed this and said that Mary Wallen had afterwards worked for her then husband. While in his employment Mary had received a letter from her uncle which she asked Mr Brereton to read for her.* When the letter was opened Anne Gent 'well remembereth there was a piece of gold of twenty shillings or two and twenty shillings as a token'. And Robert had said in the letter that 'he was sensible of the meane and low condition of the said Mary Wallen at that tyme, but wyshed her to have a good heart for that she should want nothinge'.

Then there were the visits which Robert Baker's two nephews, William and John, sons of William the Taunton mercer, had paid to London. After their father's death they had gone to Wellington and worked there as journeymen for John Hayne, a shoemaker. Hayne, aged seventy-four, now gave evidence for the first time. He stated that during the five or six years that they had worked for him they 'would be often speaking of theire unkle the said Robert Baker of Pickadilly, and of the wealth, Riches and estate that he had gotten'. And 'being as he conceiveth incuraged by hopes of some preferment to be obtayned from their said Unkle, [they] went from the Towne of Wellington in the best habitt they could then furnish themselves withall to goe and visit the said Robert Baker, theire unkle att Pickadilly at London, who received and entertained them, . . . as they themselves at their retorne home related, with much kindnesse, freindshipp and affecion as his brother's children, . . . and in token of his respects to them he did bestowe upon them moneyes, both silver and gold, as they affirmed'.

Whatever may have happened at Piccadilly Hall, old Mr Hayne was at any rate positive that they had 'returned home furnished with silver and gold', and so was Thomas Syle, who had also worked for Hayne as a journeyman. He too remembered how William and John Baker had forever been gossipping in the workshop about their famous uncle in London – they 'spake much of his wealth and Riches, which they said

* Robert Baker had dined with Mr Brereton and made the joke about the tip and the horn of the mutton which he was carving.

he had gotten by makeing of Pickadilly Collers', and they had hoped 'to gett some pre-ferrment or advantage from their said Rich uncle'. Accordingly they had 'furnished themselves with as good habits as they could provide and soe went from Wellington' to London. They had been most anxious to make a good impression, so they had 'sent up theire Cloakes by the carryer, that they might come the more handsomer unto theire said uncle's presence'. And there was no doubt that they had returned with silver and gold.

Mary Wallen, sister of William and John, said that John had lived for some time at Piccadilly Hall. John's widow, Elizabeth, who had testified before and now lived at Staplegrove with her daughter, Amye Gardiner, had evidently become rather disillus-ioned with her husband's rich uncle. Shortly after her marriage her husband had 'putt himselfe into a very good habitt and went to visitt his said uncle', who had indeed in-vited him and his wife to live at Piccadilly. There had been several visits; on one of them Robert had told his nephew that 'in regard he was then ingaged in building he could not doe much for him at that tyme', and on another occasion he had said he 'would have done more for him than he did but that he had then lately married or was upon marrying out a daughter'.* There always seemed to be an excuse why he could not help his poor relations.

Elizabeth Baker's daughter, Amye Gardiner, wife of the minister of Staplegrove, had testified in 1658 about her visit to the Widow Baker at Piccadilly Hall; now she told the same story again. When she called at the house 'the first tyme and enquired after her of her servant, she could not be admitted to come to speake with her'. But when she called a second time she had been 'invited to come into her house and had into a Roome and there attended the coming of the said Mary Baker from her chamber, she being not then ready, it being in the morning'. After 'some short tyme' Widow Baker came in and Amye had told her that she was a kinswoman of Robert Baker's. The Widow had 'at first looked very strangely' upon young Amye and had 'asked her how she should know that she . . . was related to the said Robert Baker'. The suspicious and hard-headed old lady had asked a great many questions about the Baker pedi-gree, to which Amye had replied satisfactorily, and at last the Widow had 'told her she had spoken the truth', and had called her 'Cousin'. Mary Baker then invited her 'to sitte downe by her and was very kinde unto her'; they had talked of family matters and Mary 'spake of some differences like to be between her' and the Huberts, whose claim to the estate was then getting under way. Finally she had suggested that if John Baker (the claimant, on whose behalf this evidence was given) 'would putt the power he had into the hands of her the said Mary Baker, if he had any, she would deale well enough with him'. All of which agrees closely with the evidence which Amye had given five years before.

No witnesses for George Baker were ever examined, and by the autumn of 1664 his suit against John Baker had fizzled out.[14] At first sight this curious interlude looks like

---

* Frances, who married Edward Hubert in 1622.

a feigned action instigated by John Baker to provide himself with an opportunity to collect and record more evidence against his real adversary James Baker. A more likely explanation is that the action was instigated by James Baker, who was also a defendant in the suit, for a similar purpose. Evidence which has not survived was indeed taken on James's behalf, and was later used against John.[15]

8 *Introducing an Artist at Foul Play*

At this unsuitably late stage of the story it is now necessary to introduce a new and vital character – Colonel Panton, the gambler. Thomas Panton was the youngest of the many children of Squire John Panton, who lived near Ashby de la Zouche in Leicestershire. He appears to have attended Charles II during his exile and enjoyed a titular colonelcy. After the Restoration he obtained a commission in the life guards and also a captaincy in the foot guards, and drew his pay from both regiments. He lived extravagantly in lodgings about the Court, 'keeping 4 or 5 footmen at once in good liveries, and eating and drinking very high, but above all, being always of an amorous disposition, he car'd not what expences he was at to carry on an intrigue of love'. These expenses were provided for by his success at the card table, where he won a great deal of money from the Dukes of Monmouth, Lauderdale and Buckingham and other courtiers. His chief speciality was hazard, but 'there was no game but what he was an absolute artist at, either upon the square *or foul play*'.[1]

By 1662 Colonel Panton had bought the lease of Simon Osbaldeston's gaming house and bowling greens on the east side of the Haymarket and set himself up as a croupier. This lease had originally been granted by Widow Baker in the 1630's and was due to expire in 1669.[2] Shortly after Panton had acquired the lease of the gaming house John Baker sold his reversionary rights in the freehold of this part of the family estate to Sir Henry Oxenden.[3] Unfortunately there was some legal flaw in Panton's lease,[2] so when discussion of its renewal began he must have had occasion to look very closely at the legal title to the house. When he found that the suit between James and John Baker had never been finally settled by a Chancery decree, and that Oxenden's right as the supposed owner of the freehold to grant a new lease was therefore open to doubt, he must have realised that a great opportunity had presented itself to him.

Precisely how Panton set about resuscitating James Baker's dormant claim for his own purposes is not known; it is of course possible that the initiative came from James Baker, not Panton, but this seems less probable. What is certain is that after more than three and a half years of inaction, James Baker's counsel suddenly applied to Chancery for permission to proceed to a fourth trial at common law, and in November 1664 their request was provisionally granted.[4]

By this time John Wescombe, John Baker's 'principal Agent and one whoe hath followed and maintayned the suit all along', had spent two thousand pounds in contesting James's claim.[5] He had acquired part of the estate from John, but if James were successful now, he would lose both the money he had spent and the land he had bought. His funds were exhausted and there were still debts to pay. But fortunately from his point of view Sir Henry Oxenden was in the same predicament. He too, by purchasing part of the estate from John, had laid out two thousand pounds which he would lose if James were to win in the end. So Wescombe and John Baker went to Oxenden and told him that they had no more money to carry on the cause, and Oxenden was forced, for the security of his own interests, 'to looke after the said Cause and the Management thereof'.[6]

The case now ceased in all but name to be John Baker versus James Baker, and became Sir Henry Oxenden versus Thomas Panton. Oxenden engaged new and much more distinguished counsel for John, including the attorney general, and at a hearing in May 1665 they induced the Lord Chancellor, the Earl of Clarendon, to rescind the order for a fourth trial.[7] But a month later James Baker's counsel contested this decision. They maintained that the estate was now worth nearly a thousand pounds per annum and that several new witnesses had been discovered. Moreover, they claimed that John Baker had paid one witness fifty pounds to give evidence on his behalf at the last trial, and that another had confessed 'on his death bedd that he was troubled in Conscience for what hee had sworne at ye tryall against the plaintiff James'. John Baker's counsel denied these allegations (which, it may be noted, were never presented as sworn affidavits), but ultimately 'after longe debate of the matter', the Court ordered that a new trial should be held at the Exchequer bar before a Middlesex jury. If the verdict were given against James, this was to be final, but if against John, he could apply for yet another trial. Both plaintiff and defendant were to inform one another of the names of any new witnesses whom they intended to call, and there were to be special precautions to ensure that the jury was impartial.[8]

The outbreak of the Great Plague in London prevented the trial being held for some months. Sir Henry Oxenden was furious at having to spend some eight hundred pounds in defence of his title, and declared that if James Baker were to win, then he, Sir Henry, 'would bring the tryall about agen and agen and would expend 5000 li in the suit'.[9] James produced a list of no fewer than sixty-eight new witnesses whom he intended to call, and John claimed that the people whom James had nominated as guarantors for John's costs in the event of his losing were all poor and therefore useless. Gradually these and other petty suits in miniature were settled – only ten new witnesses could be called by either side, and Ambrose Smith, a goldsmith of Devizes, stood surety for James – and eventually all was ready for the last decisive trial.[10]

A day or two before the trial two things happened. John Baker, penniless as ever, was forced to sell more of the estate to Oxenden for only two hundred pounds. Oxenden's purpose was to recoup his expenses by acquiring what would be a splendid investment if John won; by purchasing before the issue had been decided he paid far less than he would have to after a favourable verdict had been given.[6] But while Oxenden was counting his chickens before they were hatched James Baker's counsel made a clever move; they obtained leave to use at the trial the evidence (now lost) which they had taken some three years before in the abortive suit of George versus James and John Baker.[11]

The trial was held at the beginning of July 1666 in the Court of Exchequer in Westminster Hall before Sir Matthew Hale,[12] who many years before had been counsel for the defence at the impeachment of Archbishop Laud. When the jury returned to the court to give their verdict the crier followed the normal procedure and called first for the plaintiff, in this case James Baker. The trial had, he thought, gone so heavily against him that he did not know what to do – whether to appear and risk the adverse verdict which would put a final irrevocable stop to his claim, or whether to suffer a non-suit and hope to be allowed to start again. The crier called for him a second time, and still he did not come. But at the third and final call he 'att last with much unwillingness did appear'. Then came the call for the defendant, John, who (perhaps we may presume) appeared quickly and confidently. And at last came the verdict – for the plaintiff, James Baker.[13]

9 *John Baker* contra mundum

Nothing is known about what had been said or who had testified at the fourth trial. Our knowledge of the evidence comes entirely from the incomplete written Chancery depositions in the Public Record Office which have already been mentioned at length. Of that method of collecting accurate information a great modern legal authority has written that 'It may be safely said that a more futile method of getting at the facts of the case, than the system in use in the Court of Chancery from the seventeenth century onwards, never existed in any mature legal system.' So in forming an opinion about this particular trial we are at a very great disadvantage.[1]

It appears to be inconceivable that the evidence of such poor, ignorant and illiterate witnesses as Mary Wallen or John Hayne the Wellington shoemaker, to name only two, could have been sheer fabrication. Yet this is what the verdict for James Baker meant. Their and much other evidence establishes, surely, the existence of a definite link between the Robert Baker of Taunton and the Robert Baker of Piccadilly Hall, and it seems impossible to resist the conclusion that they were, indeed one and the same person.

Fortunately there is one piece of entirely independent contemporary evidence which supports this view and may be mentioned now. Edward Hubert, to whom Robert Baker's eldest daughter Frances had been married in 1622, possessed a coat of arms, and when the heralds from the College of Arms made their visitation of the county of Essex, where many of the Huberts lived, they drew up a pedigree of the family. This pedigree appears to date from about the middle of the seventeenth century and is now in the British Museum. In it Edward Hubert is described as having married Frances, daughter of Robert Baker *of Taunton*. The heralds, at least, had no doubt about his place of origin.[2]

Nor had John Baker. He kept up the struggle to vindicate his rights for the remaining fifteen years of his life. For almost the whole of his adult life he had to live with the perpetually receding prospect of vast wealth dangled before him; large sums of money had passed through his hands during the piecemeal sale of his reversionary rights, yet he had never enjoyed them and was perpetually poor. He might well have been happier if he had never heard of his rich great-uncle and had remained at his shoemaker's last in Wellington.

Within a few days of the fatal verdict at Westminster Hall his counsel applied to Chancery for a fifth trial. The verdict had been given not only against the expectation of James Baker himself and of his counsel,[3] but 'contrary to the direction of the Court and beyond the expectation of most persons that heard the Evidence of both sides'.[4] John Baker's counsel maintained that as both he and James now had a verdict and a non-suit against the other, 'the title now stands as if there had been noe tryall in the Case'. They therefore asked for a new trial, to be held before 'a Jury of a Forraigne Countye' [3] – i.e. not a Middlesex jury – for Colonel Panton, to whom James Baker was firmly engaged, 'had great interest in the County of Middlesex'.[4] The implication was that Panton, who, it will be remembered, was an absolute artist in foul play at the card table, had corrupted the jury at the last trial.

James Baker, or rather the lawyers whom Panton employed on his behalf, were too clever to oppose this application, provided, significantly, that the next trial was again held before a Middlesex jury. Lord Chancellor Clarendon, who presided at the hearing, nevertheless ordered that an Essex jury should hear the case, so James's lawyers, who perhaps thought that this would be fatal to their cause, refused to proceed with the preparatory formalities and had John Baker arrested for debt.[5] James Baker was packed off to his farm in Somerset so that his lawyers could plead that they had no instructions from their nominal client, and John was forced to the unusual step of addressing a petition to the Lord Chancellor for redress.[6] But before the matter could be disentangled the Great Fire of London threw all public business into a turmoil.

Meanwhile James, on the strength of the Exchequer verdict, had started to sell some of the land which John had sold three years before. He sold the two houses in the Strand to a carpenter, and he persuaded Dr Edmund Vintner, who had already paid John £180 for some land near Piccadilly, to pay him another £100 for the same ground.[7] But nobody would buy from John Baker now. He could not even pay James Baker's costs at the last trial, and Sir Henry Oxenden, despite his previous fulminations, was unwilling 'to run the hazard of another Tryall'.[4] So there was a short uneasy pause.

As long as the possibility of a fifth trial existed James Baker's title was as much open to doubt as John's had previously been. In due course Panton realised that John Baker had neither money nor a patron to enable him to proceed to another trial, and in November 1667 he caused James's counsel to apply in Chancery for an order to compel John to go to trial.[8] John was broke. Six weeks passed, and nothing happened. Then in February 1668 James's lawyers demanded that in default of action by John the cause should be taken as having been tried against him, and that therefore the court should issue a decree settling the matter once and for all. And so, as often happened in Chancery, the suit was won and lost because one party's purse was longer than the other's; for the Lord Keeper, Sir Orlando Bridgeman, who presided at this hearing, after 'considering how vexatious the suite hath beene', did 'order and decree that the said last Verdict doe stand, and that the said plaintiff James Baker, his heires and assignes, doe and shall accordingly hold and enjoy the said Messuages, Lands and Tenements in question with the appurtenances against the said John Baker and all claymeing by, from or under him as the sole and undoubted right heire' of Robert Baker.[9]

Two months later Widow Baker died at Piccadilly Hall, and was buried at St Martin in the Fields on 6 April 1668.[10] Throughout the forty-five years of her widowhood she had successfully maintained her hold on what she claimed as her share of the estate. She, if anyone, must have known the truth about her husband's relations, and whether James or John Baker was the imposter. Yet throughout the whole suit, and despite the pressure brought to bear on her by both claimants, she kept her peace and gave no evidence. How she was able to do this is a mystery, but in a civil suit such as this she may have been able to plead that by testifying she might prejudice her own interests.

Widow Baker's death both complicated and simplified the situation. It will be remembered that in 1622 Robert Baker had married his daughter Frances, a child by his first wife, to Edward Hubert, and that in the 1640s and 1650s the Huberts had unsuccessfully claimed all or part of the estate. Early in 1666 Edward Hubert, Frances's son, had revived his claim on fresh grounds.[11] He maintained that shortly before his mother's marriage in 1622 Robert Baker had executed a deed settling his estate on his wife Mary for life, and thereafter upon their children, if any, and in default of survivors then upon the children of his first wife. The will which Baker had made shortly before his death was, according to Hubert, either a forgery or else had been 'unduly obteyned from him in his great necessitie and sickness'.[12] As Edward Hubert was the only surviving grandchild of Robert Baker, he claimed to be the right heir.

So long as Widow Baker was alive there was not much point in pursuing this claim, so the Huberts held their fire while James and John Baker did battle in Westminster Hall. They attended all four trials, and at one of them Edward even gave evidence, though to what purpose is not known.[12] But after the widow's death they revived their suit and obtained an order against both James and John Baker for a trial in King's Bench, at which Edward Hubert was non-suited.[13] He at once demanded and was granted another trial,[12] but he died shortly afterwards, and as his son was a minor the claim lapsed again – for a while.

After Widow Baker's death her life interest in part of the estate passed to Sir Henry Oxenden for the duration of his life. Soon after the Exchequer trial James Baker had conveyed part of the estate to Colonel Panton, 'who manages the said James Baker's pretences'. With Widow Baker out of the way it was not long before Panton and Oxenden 'came to understand one another's interests better'. They agreed between themselves to divide the land on the east side of the Haymarket, and soon afterwards building development in the area of Panton and Oxenden Streets began. (None of the original houses now survive.)

The title to the estate had now become so complicated that it is quite impossible to unravel the details of it. It is, however, interesting that even after the Chancery decree in favour of James Baker, the claims of John Baker could still not be disregarded. If he had any money he might well have been able to have the decree set aside, and even without any money he could still be dangerous if he found a patron to take Oxenden's place. For a short while it seemed as if he had indeed found such a person. In 1665

John, Lord Berkeley of Stratton had begun to build himself a mansion near the site of Berkeley and Stratton Streets. He had fought with Sir Ralph Hopton for King Charles in the West Country during the Civil War; he was a Somerset man by birth, and vastly rich. He was interested in purchasing land in the outskirts of London and offered to buy up all the interests of Oxenden, Panton and both James and John Baker in the whole estate.

First of all the legal position had to be investigated. One complication could be removed if John Baker would hand over all such deeds and evidences as he possessed, and would agree to the enrollment of the Chancery decree in favour of James Baker, thereby making the revision of this decision extremely difficult. At a general conference at which both the Bakers, Oxenden, Panton and Berkeley were all represented, John Baker agreed to do this, and to relinquish all his rights in any of the estate. He was to be paid £750, two-thirds of which was to be settled on his wife and children to prevent his using it himself 'to make new troubles in the Estate'. In due course he wrote his laboured signature to the necessary agreement and the decree was enrolled.[4]

But the ink was hardly dry before Lord Berkeley changed his mind. The Huberts' claim to the whole estate (described above) had suddenly come to life again, they had not been represented at the conference, his lordship took fright and John Baker was brusquely informed 'to his utter ruine that the said Lord Berkeley would not proceed in his purchase'.[4]

We have seen that the enrollment of the Chancery decree in favour of James had made it very difficult for John to re-open the original suit, and that subsequently he had handed over his deeds and signed away all his claim to the estate. James Baker, Oxenden and Panton were not philanthropists; yet even now, with these formidable defences against John in their possession, they still feared the possibility of his trying to revive his claim. So they mortgaged part of the estate for five hundred pounds and Panton as paymaster dolled out the income to him at irregular intervals.[14]

This is an appropriate moment to refer to a matter which may well be explicable as pure chance, or which may have a more sinister meaning. James Baker claimed the Piccadilly estate as great-nephew of Robert Baker of Old Cleeve, but his ancestry cannot now be verified because the parish registers of Old Cleeve do not survive anterior to 1660. John Baker claimed as great-nephew of Robert Baker of Taunton St James, and this cannot be satisfactorily verified either because the registers do not survive anterior to 1610. From internal evidence contained in the later volumes it is certain that the register of Taunton St James for the years before 1610 was already lost at least two hundred years ago, and very possibly even earlier. The first register of Staplegrove, on the other hand, which contains proof of the existence of Robert Baker's father, William, does survive, the first entry dating from 1558. We know that James Baker went to Staplegrove to try to examine this register, but that Amye Gardiner refused to let him see it. So it is likely that he also looked at the registers of Old Cleeve and Taunton St James. Could it be that he stole them when he had seen what they contained?

With John Baker now safely under his thumb James could sell the estate at a good price, though possession was still subject to Oxenden's life interest. Panton bought the ground on the east side of the Haymarket for £1500 and ground near Picadilly Hall for £600 – no doubt these figures being much less than the real value of the lands;[15] the six acres in the vicinity of Golden Square which John had previously sold to John Wescombe now went to James Axtell, a property speculator;[16] another three acres around Marshall Street were bought by the Earl of Craven,[17] and the Blue Mews to the south of Leicester Square, where building development was now complete, went to a Kentish gentleman for £4500.[18] Between 1669 and 1673 James Baker received a total of at least £8500 from these and other sales.

At this point one might expect that John Baker would have abandoned the struggle. There was an enrolled decree in Chancery against him, he had signed away his claim (perhaps through trickery or perhaps through his own ignorance), and now James had sold the most valuable parts of the estate. Moreover his original patron, John Wescombe, was now dead.[19]

But it is very difficult for a man to cease striving to gain something which he knows should in justice be his. The sense of injustice is never absent for long, and the thought that others are in luxurious enjoyment of the estate can become a constantly recurring torment for which renewed action – any action, however futile – provides the only relief. What John Baker needed, as always, was money. Lack of money had in the end been the principal cause of his defeat, and only by getting hold of some money of his own could he hope to reverse the Chancery decree. So in 1673 he started a new suit in which he alleged that he was entitled to receive payment of the five hundred-pound fund which Panton, Oxenden and James Baker had set aside for the purpose of keeping him quiet.[4] If he could establish that he had a legal right to this money and that it had not been just a contemptuous sop provided to keep him from starving, the corollary of such recognition would be that he also still had legal rights in the estate as Robert Baker's heir. Then, with the five hundred pounds available to pay his costs, he would be able to set about the task of having the Chancery decree rescinded and finally vindicating his title against James Baker.

The contest lasted for eight years. John Baker's only supporter was his wife, who seems to have had a good business head,[4] and against him were the formidable trio of Panton, Oxenden and James Baker. At first the latter did not take John's new suit very seriously, and busied himself with the Huberts' claim, which was finally abandoned in 1680.[20] He was also having trouble with the Pantons, for the colonel's brother, Edward, tried to get hold of part of the estate by fraud.[21] Meanwhile, after many delays, John Baker's cause came on for final decision by the Lord Chancellor, Lord Nottingham.

Lord Nottingham was one of the great Lord Chancellors, comparable in stature with later holders of the Great Seal such as Hardwicke and Eldon. He had played no part in the earlier suit between James and John Baker, or in the four Common Law trials, and so he could approach the subject unprejudiced by previous events. Now, on 15 December 1681, he gave judgment for the plaintiff, and Colonel Panton was ordered to pay John Baker the five hundred pounds plus interest.[22]

So at last, despite all the evasion, trickery and fraud that had been practised against him, the existence of John Baker's rights was recognised once more, and with money of his own he could start afresh to win back his inheritance. Panton paid four days later, on 19 December.[22] But the shock of final triumph, after nearly twenty-five years of frustration and disappointment, was too great for John Baker. He died a few hours later, far from his West Country home and family, and was buried on 23 December at St Martin in the Field, the last resting place of so many of the descendants of the tailor of Piccadilly Hall.[10]

He had composed his will a few weeks earlier, when the outcome of the suit was still uncertain. Firstly, he wrote, 'I bequeath and surrender willingly and in all humility my Soule unto Almighty God, from whome I received it, and my Body to the Earth to bee decently buried'. His wife had evidently died recently, so he bequeathed all his 'Worldly Estate, wherewith God of his infinite goodness hath invested mee and bestowed upon mee' to his only daughter, Martha, and her heirs, or in default of heirs to his 'Loving Brother', Roger, and his heirs. And if Roger had no heirs, then 'to my right heires for ever' – let them fight it out, whoever they might be.[23]

None of the principal figures in John Baker's life outlived him for long. James Baker died in 1684. In his will he only made cursory acknowledgment of his Creator before proceeding to the more important business of arranging for his earthly estate, all of which he bequeathed to his wife, Grace.[24] Colonel Panton died a year later and was buried in Westminster Abbey. In one night's gambling he had won enough money to buy an estate in Herefordshire worth fifteen hundred pounds a year, and thereafter he abjured all games of chance.

Sir Henry Oxenden took a third wife, and by the time of his death in 1686, aged seventy-two, the memory of his first brief marriage with Mary Baker fifty years before must have become very dim. Aldred Seaman died in the next year, aged seventy-eight, and was buried in Milverton church, where a stone in the chancel floor still commemorates him.[25] So now only James Baker's wife Grace survived. She was perhaps a Londoner by birth, for after her husband's death she left Evercreech and lived in the parish of St Andrew's, Holborn. She was comfortably off, and when she died, at a great age, in 1706, she bequeathed what was left of the estate to two friends, whom she appointed as her executors.[26]

But this was not quite the end of the story. The right heirs whom John Baker had mentioned in his will did not abandon their claim. Already they had been harrying Grace Baker, and after her death they claimed possession of some houses in Wardour Street.[27] By this time almost all of Robert Baker's lands had been built over, and hundreds of leasehold interests had been created. The estate had grown enormously in value – in 1695 the Blue Mews alone was worth over eleven thousand pounds [28] – and so, too, had grown the difficulty of recovering it. Nevertheless some forty years after John Baker's death one Philip Baker of Taunton still thought it worth his while to carry on the struggle, and in 1720 he bought out the rival interests of two Bakers, both yeomen living at Old Cleeve and probably collateral descendants of James Baker.[29] How Philip Baker fared with his claim has not been discovered.

There is much else throughout the long tangled story that has not been discovered. Perhaps in years to come some other student may find new evidence at the Public Record Office, where, we may confidently assume, there is still much to be found. In London there is no visible survival of the Bakers' residence – not so much as a commemorative plaque – and even the site of Piccadilly Hall on the east side of Great Windmill Street can only be roughly conjectured. But in Somerset the situation is the reverse. The chances of finding fresh written records there seem small, but the remote presence of the Bakers can still be apprehended at Chidgley or Leighland, the ancestral home of the Old Cleeve family, or in the parish church of St Andrew, where a seventeenth-century alms-box beside the door bears the inscription which James must have read as a boy before he went to live at Stratton near Evercreech – 'Remember ye poore. Bee mercifull after thy power. He that hath pitie upon ye poore leadeth unto the Lord'.

Today no Baker lives at Old Cleeve or Stratton, but it is still a common name in Taunton. There, on the north wall of the great spacious church of St Mary Magdalene, is the splendid life-size effigy of Robert Gray, a contemporary of Robert Baker who went to London to make his fortune, and who, unlike Baker, returned to found an almshouse and die in his native town. Their careers were very similar, and they must surely have known one another. There may, too, have been a general resemblance of dress and figure. Here, standing before the Gray memorial in St Mary's, we can glimpse Robert Baker's outward aspect from the effigy of his contemporary, with the heavy worsted gown, the tasselled square-toed shoes, white cuffs and piccadilly collar, and the little pointed beard and grave, heavily lined face.

If we leave Taunton by the Wellington road we come, after some five miles, to a road leading to Nynehead. Close beside the corner stands an unremarkable house until recently used as a road house, and called the Piccadilly Café. Over a century ago this house was known as the Piccadilly Inn, and the land on either side of it was then owned by William and Thomas Baker.[30] Some two hundred years previously John Baker's patron, John Wescombe, had lived nearby at Hillfarance. There are still half a dozen Bakers in this vicinity.

If we go two miles further down the road from Taunton, along the highway which Robert Baker's orphaned nephews, the journeymen shoemakers, trod, we come to Wellington. Here live some fifty Bakers. Perhaps none of them are descendants of John Baker – it is impossible to find out for certain one way or the other. Whoever his descendants may be, we may hope that they are contented and prosperous, still living and working in the fields and hills and little towns of Somerset.

1 *The Bakers of Staplegrove*

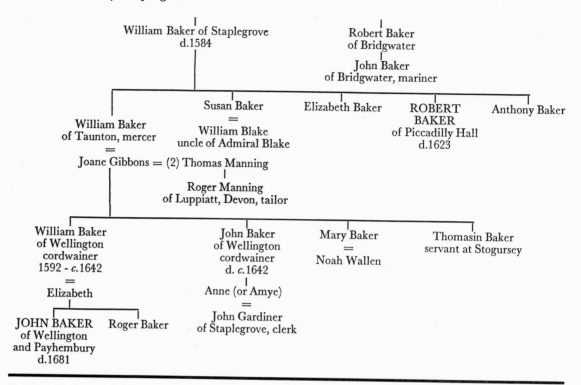

2 *The Bakers of Piccadilly*

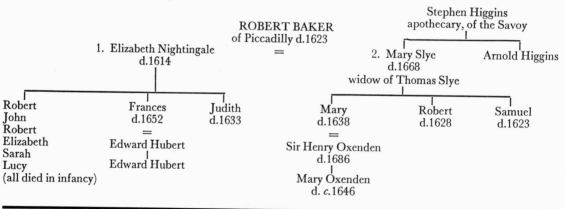

3 *The Bakers of Old Cleeve*

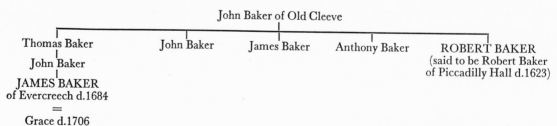

References

Abbreviations

PRO   Public Record Office.
SRO   Somerset Record Office.
WCL   Westminster City Library, Buckingham Palace Road.

Chapter 1 – Robert Baker the Tailor

1. *Notes and Queries*, third series, vol. IX, 1866, pp. 176, 249, 329.
2. T. Blount, *Glossographia: or A Dictionary, Interpreting all such Hard Words*, 1656.
3. Peter Cunningham, *A Handbook for London*, 1849, vol. II, pp. 654-5.
4. C. L. Kingsford, *The Early History of Piccadilly, Leicester Square, Soho and Their Neighbourhood*, 1925, pp. 72-3.
5. Noel Blakiston, 'The Origin of Piccadilly', in *Notes and Queries*, vol. 187, 1944, pp. 24-7.
6. *Survey of London*, vol. XXXI, 1963, pp. 32-40.
7. PRO, C10/76/10.
8. *Ibid.*, C22/762/17.
9. SRO, parish registers of Staplegrove.
10. Parish registers of St Mary Magdalene, Taunton.
11. SRO Taunton (late) Priory surrenders, 4 Oct. 41 Eliz.
12. PRO, C3/234/31: SRO., Taunton (late) Priory surrenders, 17 Jan. 26 Eliz.: John Collinson, *History of Somerset*, 1791, vol. III, p. 233.
13. PRO, C3/234/31; C22/767/37, evidence of Mary Wallen.
14. *Ibid.*, C3/234/31.
15. *Ibid.*, C22/767/37.
16. Joshua Toulmin, *The History of the Town of Taunton*, ed. J. Savage, 1822, p. 374n.
17. PRO, C24/836, no. 8.
18. *Ibid.*, Req 2/392/1.
19. *Ibid.*, C24/836, no. 8; C22/762/17.
20. WCL, parish registers of St Martin in the Fields (*Pubs. Harleian Society*, vol. XXV, 1898, p. 84).
21. *Ibid.*, (pp. 31, 32, 146).
22. WCL, F330.
23. *Ibid.*, F330: PRO, C24/836, no. 8.
24. *Survey of London*, vol. XVIII, 1937, pp. 53-9.
25. WCL, parish registers of St Martin in the Fields (*Pubs. Harleian Society*, vol. XXV, 1898, pp. 35, 38, 39, 41, 44, 159, 163, 164, 167, 169).
26. *Survey of London*, vol. XVIII, 1937, pp. 94-6: *Stowe's Chronicle*, 1632 ed., p. 894.
27. Mary Anne Everett Green, *Elizabeth, Electress Palatine and Queen of Bohemia*, 1909 ed., chapter I.
28. PRO, E351/3087, accounts of Lord Hay.
29. *Ibid.*, E407/57.

Chapter 2 – Robert Baker the Speculative Builder

1. *Survey of London*, vol. **xxxi**, 1963, pp. 35-6.
2. PRO, C24/836, no. 8.
3. *Survey of London*, vol. **xxxi**, 1963, p. 36.
4. PRO, PROB 11/141/54, will of Robert Baker.
5. PRO, E317/Midd. 73.
6. WCL, parish registers of St Martin in the Fields (*Pubs. Harleian Society*, vol. **xxv**, 1898, p. 169).
7. *Ibid.*, (p. 97).
8 *Survey of London*, vol. **xxxi**, 1963, p. 34.
9. For the following paragraphs see *Survey of London*, vol. **xxxi**, 1963, pp. 34-5, and Robert Steele, *Tudor and Stuart Proclamations, 1485-1714*, 1910, *passim*.
10. *Survey of London*, vol. **xxxi**, p. 35.
11. PRO, Sta Cha 8/30/17.
12. *Ibid.*, C6/169/66: *Survey of London*, vol. **xxxi**, 1963, pp. 24-5, 44.
13. PRO, C22/762/17.
14. WCL, parish registers of St Martin in the Fields (*Pubs. Harleian Society*, vol. **xxv**, 1898, p. 49, and vol. 66, 1936, pp. 5, 19).
15. PRO, C8/85/137; C9/38/21.
16. WCL, parish registers of St Martin the Fields (*Pubs. Harleian Society*, vol. 66, 1936, p. 178); churchwardens' accounts.

Chapter 3 – Mary Baker's Inheritance

1. PRO, PROB 11/141/54, will of Robert Baker.
2. WCL, parish registers of St Martin in the Fields (*Pubs. Harleian Society*, vol. 66, 1936, p. 179).
3. PRO, C8/85/137.
4. *Ibid.*, PROB 11/143/12, will of Samuel Baker.
5. *Ibid.*, C2/Jas. I, B29/43.
6. *Ibid.*, PROB 11/143/12, will of Samuel Baker; PROB 11/176/12, will of Gregory Baker.
7. *Ibid.*, Wards 5/26.
8. *Ibid.*, Wards 4/14.
9. William Knowles, *The Earl of Strafforde's Letters*, 1739, vol. **ii**, p. 150.
10. PRO, SP16/461, no. 95.
11. *Ibid.*, SP16/408, no. 178.
12. *Ibid.*, SP16/389, no. 85.
13. *Ibid.*, PC2/50, p. 477; PC2/51, pp. 61-2.
14. *The Oxinden Letters 1607-1642*, ed. Dorothy Gardiner, 1933, *passim*.
15. PRO, C6/143/38.
16. *Ibid.*, PROB 11/164/61, will of Judith Baker.
17. *Ibid.*, C8/70/94; C10/42/129.
18. *Ibid.*, C10/471/80.
19. *Ibid.*, C33/203, f.1274; C33/205, ff.425, 690.
20. *Ibid.*, C22/767/37.
21. *Ibid.*, C22/762/17.

Chapter 4 – The Court of Chancery

1. Sir William Holdsworth, *A History of English Law*, vol. **i**, 1903.
2. *Ibid.*, vol. **i**, p. 245.
3. *Lord Nottingham's Manual of Chancery Practice*, ed. D. E. C. Yale, 1965, p. 63.

4. PRO, C33/207, f.1135.
5. *Ibid.,* C8/285/13.
6. *Ibid.,* C31/34, Trin. 1660, no. 125: John Collinson, *History of Somerset,* 1791, vol. III, pp. 17-18.
7. Collinson, 1791, vol. III, pp. 18, 527-8.
8. PRO, C31/34, Trin. 1660, no. 123.
9. *Ibid.,* PROB 11/337/109, will of John Wescombe.
10. *Ibid.,* C54/4142, no. 4.
11. *Ibid.,* C33/209, f.514.
12. *Ibid.,* C10/76/10.
13. *Ibid.,* C33/209, f.1197.
14. *Ibid.,* C33/211, f.184.
15. *Ibid.,* C38/154.
16. *Ibid.,* C33/209, f.796.
17. *Ibid.,* C22/15/40.
18. *Lord Nottingham's Manual, ut supra,* p. 107.
19. PROB 11/78/83, will of John Baker.

Chapter 5 – A Long Day at the Fountain in Taunton

1. Unless otherwise stated, all the evidence in this chapter is based on PRO, C22/762/17.
2. SRO, Taunton (late) Priory surrenders, 17 Jan. 26 Eliz.
3. *Ibid.,* Taunton (late) Priory surrenders, 4 Oct. 41 Eliz.
4. Parish registers of St Mary Magdalene, Taunton.

Chapter 6 – The Case Comes On

1. PRO, C24/836, no. 8.
2. WCL, parish registers of St Martin in the Fields (*Pubs. Harleian Society,* vol. **xxv**, 1898, p. 73).
3. PRO, PROB 11/164/61, will of Judith Baker.
4. WCL, parish registers of St Martin in the Fields (*Pubs. Harleian Society,* vol. **xxv**, 1898, p. 84).
5. Joshua Toulmin, *The History of Taunton,* ed. James Savage, 1822, pp. 4-5.
6. PRO, C24/835, no. 11.
7. *Ibid.,* C33/211, f.850: Greater London Record Office, E/Bur/349.
8. PRO, C31/34, Trin. 1660, nos. 53, 123, 125-6.
9. *Ibid.,* C31/34, Trin. 1660, no. 54.
10. *Ibid.,* C31/34, Trin. 1660, no. 123: Jacob's *Law Dictionary,* 1809, vol. II, *sub* non suit and privy verdict.
11. PRO, C33/213, ff.8, 167, 286.
12. *Ibid.,* C31/34, Trin. 1660, no. 114.
13. *Ibid.,* C33/213, f.402.
14. *Ibid.,* C31/34, Mich. 1660, no. 324.
15. *Ibid.,* C31/34, Mich. 1660, no. 242.
16. *Ibid.,* C31/34, Mich. 1660, no. 291.
17. *Ibid.,* C31/34, Mich. 1660, no. 282.
18. *Ibid.,* C33/215, ff.120, 149, 169, 329.
19. *Ibid.,* C33/215, f.525.

Chapter 7 – The Break-up of the Estate

1. PRO, C54/4137, no. 5.
2. *Ibid.,* C8/285/13.

3. *Ibid.*, C54/4139, no. 9.
4. *Ibid.*, C54/4141, no. 9.
5. *Ibid.*, C54/4142, no. 5.
6. *Ibid.*, C54/4166, no. 4.
7. *Ibid.*, C54/4166, no. 3; C54/4168, no. 26.
8. *Ibid.*, C54/4169, no. 19.
9. *Ibid.*, C54/4142, no. 4.
10. *Ibid.*, C33/219, f.846.
11. *Ibid.*, C41/16, Mich. 1663, nos. 944, 1104, 1105.
12. *Ibid.*, C33/221, ff.196, 428; C38/146.
13. This and the next five paragraphs are based on PRO, C22/767/37.
14. *Ibid.*, C33/221, ff.901, 1023.
15. *Ibid.*, C33/225, f.403.

Chapter 8 – Introducing an Artist at Foul Play

1. *Games and Gamesters of the Restoration*, introd. C. H. Hartmann, 1930, pp. 153-8: *Dictionary of National Biography*.
2. PRO, C8/244/79.
3. *Ibid.*, C54/4142, no. 5.
4. *Ibid.*, C33/223, f.226.
5. *Ibid.*, C33/223, f.721.
6. *Ibid.*, C8/285/13.
7. *Ibid.*, C33/223, f.519.
8. *Ibid.*, C33/223, ff.721, 760.
9. *Ibid.*, C41/17, Trin. 1666, nos. 569-70; C8/285/13.
10. *Ibid.*, C33/223, f.756; C33/225, f.182; C38/154; C38/156.
11. *Ibid.*, C33/225, f.403.
12. Greater London Record Office, E/Bur/358/2.
13. PRO, C33/225, f.424.

Chapter 9 – John Baker contra mundum

1. *Lord Nottingham's Manual of Chancery Practice*, ed. D. E. C. Yale, 1965, p. 58, quoting Sir William Holdsworth.
2. British Museum, Dept. of MSS., Harleian MS. 1541, p. 198b, printed in *Pubs. Harleian Society*, vol. xiv, 1879, p. 584.
3. PRO, C33/225, f.424.
4. *Ibid.*, C8/285/13.
5. *Ibid.*, C33/225, ff.406, 424.
6. *Ibid.*, C41/17, Trin. 1666, nos. 802-3; C33/225, f.406.
7. *Ibid.*, C54/4196, no. 22; C54/4197, no. 32; C54/4198, no. 20.
8. *Ibid.*, C33/229, f.111.
9. *Ibid.*, C33/229, f.338.
10. WCL, parish registers of St Martin in the Fields.
11. PRO, C33/229, f.640.
12. *Ibid.*, C33/231, f.406.
13. *Ibid.*, C33/229, f.719; C33/231, f.175.
14. *Ibid.*, C33/255, ff.442-3.
15. *Ibid.*, C54/4383, nos. 28-32.
16. *Ibid.*, C54/4382, no. 25.

17. *Ibid.*, C54/4315, no. 14.
18. *Ibid.*, C54/4317, no. 24.
19. *Ibid.*, PROB 11/337/109, will of John Wescombe.
20. *Ibid.*, C33/253, ff.270, 407, 482.
21. *Ibid.*, C33/253, f.141.
22. *Ibid.*, C33/257, f.80.
23. *Ibid.*, PROB 11/368/179, will of John Baker.
24. *Ibid.*, PROB 11/376/54, will of James Baker.
25. John Collinson, *History of Somerset*, vol. III, 1791, pp. 17-18.
26. PRO, PROB 11/490/190, will of Grace Baker.
27. *Ibid.*, C10/389/13.
28. *Ibid.*, C5/313/38.
29. Greater London Record Office, Middlesex Deeeds Registry 1720/5/230-1.
30. Tithe map and schedule of the parish of West Buckland.

Index

The abbreviation R. B. denotes Robert Baker of Piccadilly Hall.

QUEEN MARY
COLLEGE
LIBRARY